KINDERTRANSPORT

OLGA LEVY DRUCKER

Kindertransport

◆ ◆ ◆

Henry Holt and Company • *New York*

Henry Holt and Company, Inc.
Publishers since 1866
115 West 18th Street
New York, New York 10011

Henry Holt is a registered
trademark of Henry Holt and Company, Inc.

Published in Canada by Fitzhenry & Whiteside Ltd.,
195 Allstate Parkway, Markham, Ontario L3R 4T8.

Library of Congress Cataloging-in-Publication Data
Drucker, Olga Levy.
    Kindertransport / Olga Drucker.
    Summary: The author describes the circumstances in Germany after Hitler
came to power that led to the evacuation of many Jewish children to England
and her experiences as a young girl in England during World War II.
    1. Drucker, Olga—Juvenile literature.   2. Jewish children—Germany—Biography—
Juvenile literature.   3. Jews—Germany—Biography—Juvenile literature.   4. Refugees,
Jewish—Great Britain—Biography—Juvenile literature.   5. Germany—Biography—
Juvenile literature.   [1. Drucker, Olga Levy.   2. Jews—Germany—Biography.
3. Refugees—Great Britain.   4. World War, 1939–1945—Personal narratives, Jewish.]
I. Title. DS135.G5D783 1992   940.53'161'092—dc20   92-14121   [B]

ISBN 0-8050-1711-9 (hardcover)
10 9 8 7 6 5 4 3
ISBN 0-8050-4251-2 (paperback)
10 9 8 7 6 5 4 3 2 1

First published in hardcover in 1992 by Henry Holt and Company, Inc.
First Owlet edition, 1995

Printed in the United States of America on acid-free paper. ∞

All survivors have a story, and there are as many stories as there are individuals who do the telling. To all those who lived to tell *their* story, and to all who did not—and to all my German-Jewish ancestors who tried for so many generations to carry on their daily lives in freedom and peace— I dedicate *my* story.

Author's Note

In the telling of my story, I have used real names only of those of my immediate family. All others have been changed. The events are true to the best of my ability to remember.

KINDERTRANSPORT

CONTENTS

1

MY HOUSE

"Why is there a tree on top of the house?"

It was winter 1932, and I was standing with my parents in the mud where a street was going to be. I pointed up at the wooden scaffolding around a three-story house. The house looked to me as if it were climbing up the side of the hill. Vineyards still grew behind it. The roof of the house was flat, and a small spruce tree seemed to be sprouting from its top. To the tree was tied a red rag that waved merrily in the cold wind, like a flag.

My brother Hans came bounding out from somewhere in back, bursting with excitement.

"There's a perfect corner for an Indian tent back there, and I saw a great place for a tree house, and—"

Mama interrupted him. "Look at your boots, Hans. Didn't I tell you to stay out of the mud?"

Hans looked guiltily down at his boots. Then he raised his curly red head and gave Mama one of those smiles of his. She never could resist them.

But my question hadn't been answered yet.

"Papa? The tree?"

"Well, it's just a custom, you see, Ollie," he said. "No one really remembers why anymore. All I know is that whenever the last nail has been hammered into the framework of a new house, the builders celebrate by placing a tree on the roof. It probably goes back to very ancient times. Anyway, it's done all over. Does that answer your question, Miss Nosyface?"

"Is it done all over the whole *world*?" I asked. Papa laughed.

"I don't know about the whole world, Ollie. All I know is it's done where we live, here in Stuttgart, Germany." Papa pulled his shoulders back and stood straighter than that little tree high up on the roof.

"It's going to be such a beautiful house," said Mama. Her eyes were shining. "We've waited so long for this. I can see it now. White stucco. Big picture window downstairs in the drawing room. I'll keep a rubber tree plant in it. It will grow and grow and climb clear across the ceiling, just like the one my aunt, Tante Julchen, had when I was a child. And we'll have a balcony all across the second floor where the bedrooms will be, and—"

"I thought you liked our apartment," teased Papa, with a perfectly straight face. I could tell how pleased he was, though, by his voice.

"Oh, I do," Mama answered quickly. "But a house. . . !

Just think, children. You'll each have your very own room!"

"And a playroom," added Papa.

"And a garden with secret hiding places," added Hans.

"And a roof that's flat with a tree on it," said I.

Everybody laughed. "Silly," said Hans. "The tree doesn't stay there." My face must have shown my disappointment. "Never mind," he tried to comfort me. "You're only five years old. When you get to be thirteen, like me, you'll know more stuff."

"She already knows a lot of stuff," said Papa. "And if you're so smart, young man, how about scraping that mud off your boots before your mother has to speak to you about it again?"

"When will our house be finished, Daddy? Will we move into it soon?" He had called him Daddy, the way English children addressed their papas. I knew he was trying to impress him. But he did start scraping his muddy boots on one of the bricks lying around. Papa sighed deeply.

"I certainly hope so," he said.

2

MOVING DAY

Moving vans finally arrived near the end of summer that same year. All our good dishes and glasses and silverware were packed in boxes. The three big oil paintings of my grandfather and his father and my great-great-grandfather were carefully wrapped in burlap to go in the van. Great-great-grandfather, Herz Levy, had lived to be a hundred and three years old, so Papa always told us. And grandfather Maximilian had been the founder of Papa's publishing firm a very long time ago, in 1871. But he and grandmother Eugenie died before I was born. I often wished I could have met them. There had even been room in the van for the grand piano and for Papa's rolltop desk and favorite leather armchair. But a lot of the heavy old dark stuff was left behind. Mama wanted only new, modern things in our new house. "They have to fit in with the modern style," she said. She picked out a lot of glass and shiny chrome and brightly upholstered furniture. Hans and I got new beds.

Everything was in a big mess, and all the adults were very busy. "Go play somewhere, children," we were told. "Stay out of the way."

"Want to explore the place?" Hans asked me. I was thrilled. It wasn't often that my big brother included me in any of his games. "We'll start in the cellar and work our way up," he informed me. I tagged along behind him.

"It's cold down here," I complained, hugging myself. "And it smells funny. What are all those bottles?"

"That's wine. Grown-ups like to drink it. When I'm grown-up, I will drink a glass for every meal." We were standing on a dirt floor. I had goose bumps on my thin arms.

"Even for breakfast?" I asked.

But he ignored my question, choosing to respond to my complaint of the cold. "It's supposed to be cold in a wine cellar. It's good for the wine."

How did he know all that? I wondered in admiration.

I skipped ahead, into another part of the cellar.

"Look, Hans. This is where Frieda can do the washing and ironing." This was something I knew about. I had watched our nanny often enough. Here was the washtub, with the corrugated washboard in it. And here, next to it, were the two heavy flat irons. I had seen Frieda use one of these on Papa's starched white shirts, while the other was heating up over a coal fire. Frieda liked to sing while she worked with the irons. Maybe it helped her forget what hard work she was doing. After all, ironing

Papa's shirts and button-on collars was only a part of her work. Frieda looked after me from morning till night. She had been my nanny for as long as I could remember.

Now Hans was pushing a door open. Sunlight came streaming through it from the garden. I followed him outside. A path led down the hill toward the street and all around the front of the house and up again on the other side, where a flight of steep steps led to the main entrance. As usual, Hans got there first. This time I tripped up the steps and scraped my knees. I didn't cry. This sort of thing happened to me almost every day. I always wore Band-Aids on my knees.

We ducked past some moving men into the front foyer.

"Better wipe our shoes off," I warned Hans, remembering. "You know how Mama feels about mud. Look! White floors!"

"What are these for?" Hans asked, pointing to a neat row of felt slippers lined up by the umbrella stand.

"I think Mama wants us to wear them in the house. So as not to scuff up her white floors."

We unlaced our shoes and stuffed our feet into the slippers.

"Wheee! You can skate in these!" cried Hans, demonstrating.

"You better not!" I giggled. "Come on. Let's go."

We found the drawing room and peeked in. The floor-to-ceiling bookshelves were still empty. But a mountain of boxes filled with books was sitting there, waiting to fill them, as you would expect in the house of a publisher. Papa and my uncle, Onkel Erich owned a company that made nothing but children's books. Grandpa Maximilian Levy had been the founder of it. Even though I was only five, I could already read some of the easier ones. I think Mama, and even Papa, were quite proud of me for that.

One of the moving men came in carrying a rubber tree plant.

"Where do you want this, ma'am?" he asked. I hadn't noticed till just then that Mama was in the room too.

"Right here on the window sill," she told him. I smiled, remembering how she had imagined her house that winter afternoon, when we were all standing outside in the mud, looking up at nothing more than a framework with a tree on top. But this plant was so tiny! How would it ever grow big enough to reach the ceiling? Would I grow bigger too someday? Just then I heard a peep. I turned and saw another moving man carrying Piepsi, our canary, inside his cage.

"And this?"

"Right under the plant," Mama directed. Piepsi began to sing.

"He likes it here," said Hans. "That's because he can look out the window."

I stepped closer. "Maybe it's because he can see our reflections in the window," I said. I was looking at Hans and myself in the glass—a lanky boy in short pants, his curly red hair a foot above the light blue ribbon tied into my own straight, blond hair; my enormous eyes matching the ribbon; my skinny legs in their brown woolen stockings, skinny arms sticking out of my flower-print cotton dress. Every night I prayed that I would soon grow taller and fatter, but so far I hadn't.

Piepsi's singing had drawn Mama's attention to us.

"I thought I told you two to stay out of the way," she scolded. We laughed and quickly ran through the open glass door that separated the drawing room from the dining room. As we ran, the movers were carrying in the piano, groaning and swearing under their breath.

"Let's get out of here," cried Hans. I followed him. Now we were in the hallway. Behind a door to the right was the downstairs bathroom. Hans went in and banged the door shut. I kept running. At the end of the hallway I found the kitchen. After a few minutes, Hans joined me there. Cook was busy putting away pots and pans. She was completely surrounded by dishes and glassware and kitchen stuff.

"Shoo! Shoo!" she cried, holding a wooden spoon over her head. "Don't get in my way. You must have something better to do than—"

"What's that big white box?" I asked, opening my eyes wide and pointing to an unfamiliar object behind her. It worked. She stopped scolding and turned around.

"What box? Oh, the ice box! Your papa got us this," she said, proud as could be. "When the man comes to put these big blocks of ice in it—up here, you see?—we can keep meat and milk and butter in it, and nothing will spoil. Not bad, huh? What won't they think of next?"

"Won't we need a pantry any more?" asked Hans. I knew he liked to steal stuff from the pantry when he thought nobody was looking. To tell the truth, so did I.

"A pantry? But of course we'll still have a pantry," said Cook. "Right over here. Who ever heard of anybody not having a pantry?" she laughed. But then she remembered again. "Now get out of here, you two *Schlingel*, before you break something. And get your hands off these wine glasses, Hans. They're your mama's best stemware. She'll have my hide if any of them break. Out!"

Hans turned to leave. But I still had something on my mind.

"Could I please have a chocolate sandwich first?" I asked, as sweetly as I could. Cook gave me a funny look.

"Later," she promised, "as soon as I can find the chocolate. Who can find anything in such a mess?"

White bread and butter with a few thin, dark chocolate wafers between the slices was my favorite treat. Cook made it for me whenever I asked her. She loved to spoil me. But now her mind was set. "Out!" she yelled, waving that wooden spoon again.

This time we both knew she meant it. We were out of there before she could throw her spoon at us.

"Race you upstairs!" cried Hans, and again I followed him. My face felt hot and sweaty with excitement. He won, of course.

We opened doors and banged them shut again. First, the guest room. Mama's sewing machine was already waiting there. So was a chest with all its drawers out on the floor. The drawers were filled with sweaters and other warm clothes. Then, my room. The closets were built in, so that they looked flat in line with the walls.

"It's a nice blue," I told Hans. "I like it. Mama said your room would be green."

It was. The big bathroom next door had a tub in it. An inside door from this bathroom led straight into our parents' room.

"They're lucky. They have a balcony," said Hans.

"So do you," I pointed out. "See, it's all one from their room to yours." I remembered Mama dreaming of a balcony that would go straight across the front of the house. We started running from one end to the other, yelling at the top of our lungs. We were making so much noise we didn't hear Frieda come up behind us.

"Stop this racket this minute!"

"Aw, Frieda! We were just—"

"Never mind what you were just. Whatever will the neighbors think of two such noisy hooligans? Anyway, it's time to wash hands for supper."

"Can we quickly go see what's up on the next floor? Please? Please?" I asked.

"Well, if you're quick. I'll give you five minutes. And stay out of my room," she called after us. We were already on our way.

Up another flight. Frieda's room. Another little bathroom. A storage room, full of unpacked boxes and travel trunks. Our playroom, where some boxes had already been opened. My brother's train set spilled out from one, his fort and lead soldiers from another. My dolls and stuffed animals and games were piled up, and some of my play dishes. And more books.

"Here's another door!" cried Hans jubilantly. "Let's see where this one leads to."

We stepped out on the roof garden. It had a tall chain link fence all around. In back was an overhang with a window, so we could look down into the garden below.

"Look, Hans. I can ride my scooter up here." I shouted.

"What scooter?"

"The one I'm getting for my birthday. And roller skates, too."

"Don't be so sure."

"You're a horrid brother!" I laughed, and I chased him down three flights of stairs. Our supper of little sausages, called *Würstchen*, and potato salad was waiting for us in the cluttered kitchen.

3

TRAINS AND SCHOOL

*O*nly a year later, when I was nearly six, Hitler became Germany's *Führer,* or Leader. At first my life did not seem to change very much.

In March 1933, Frieda took me on a train to her village, Ochsenbach, to her family's farm. Her mother and father and two brothers lived in two rooms built over the cow barn. Their windows looked directly into the barnyard, which was dominated by a great huge dung heap. Hens and geese scratched happily around it all day. On its peak stood the rooster, tall and proud in his iridescent greens and blues, his red comb reaching as far as the sky itself as he crowed to his heart's delight.

When Frieda's mother first saw me, she said: "Skinny little thing. We'll have to fatten her up, won't we?"

At home I had always been a fussy eater. I also knew very well what happened to Hansel and Gretel in the fairy tale when the witch fattened them up! Despite all that, I began to stuff myself. I drank fresh milk, still warm from the cow that I had watched Frieda's brother tend. I ate home-churned butter, which I had helped churn. And I gobbled up the eggs, which I had helped collect from wherever the hens had decided to lay them. I was never happier, and I considered the smell of the dung heap more wonderful than Mama's perfume. My thin face began to fill out, my cheeks grew rosy, and I shot up several inches.

But only a few weeks later, I came down with whooping cough. The doctor said a few days in the Black Forest would cure me. Off we went, Mama and I, on yet another train. I loved train rides. Every day, Mama and I sat under the sweet-smelling pine trees on the soft needles that had dropped off their branches. She showed me how to make little baskets out of the grasses that grew nearby.

Then I collected pine cones, into which we wedged chocolate candy called nonpareils, and placed them into the baskets. These became coming-home presents for Papa, Hans, Frieda and Cook.

My cough quickly got better. Mama and I looked forward to our trip back to Stuttgart. But our coming home was not as joyous as we had expected. On our return, our family and friends were talking about nothing but the boycott.

This boycott, we learned, was organized as a nationwide action by the Nazis to prevent German non-Jews from buying or selling goods in Jewish owned stores. Hitler's storm-troopers, called S.A. for *Sturm Abteilung*, went so far as to beat up would-be shoppers who tried to defy his orders. At about that time, signs began to appear in windows of non-Jewish stores which read "Jews are not wanted as customers here." Some German shop owners omitted the signs at the risk of also being beaten up by the S.A. But most took heed. Either they were afraid, or they disliked Jews themselves. It was at about that time, it seemed to me, that Papa started to become preoccupied. He didn't always hear what I said to him, and he seemed to get annoyed with me more quickly. But he still went to his office every day and came home for lunch as before.

♦　♦　♦

That summer I traveled with my family to Switzerland. This time the train took us into long tunnels dug straight through the mountains. When we came out at the other end, we saw that many of the mountains had snow on top, even though it was the middle of July. While Papa and Hans hiked up mountain trails, Mama, Frieda, and I took walks about town or had picnics in the meadow. I learned to make daisy chains, which I wore on my head like a crown. In our hotel I slept in a brass bed. I called it my "golden bed."

No sooner were we home in Stuttgart again than Hans and I were packed off to summer camp. For me it was the first time.

"But I'd rather stay home!" I wailed. "Why do I have to go to summer camp?"

"You'll like it there," Mama promised me.

Hans said, "It's just so Mama and Papa can be without us for a bit." This did nothing to calm me. But, I thought, he must have understood such things better. He was fourteen now.

"Why do they want to be alone without us? It's much more fun when we're all together," I insisted.

Nothing helped. Our bags, so recently unpacked, were packed again, this time with new camp clothes. All had our names sewn into them.

The day before we were supposed to leave, I sat my dolls around my toy table and held one last tea party for them.

"Now don't you cry when I'm away," I told them. "I'll be back before you know it." I hugged each one in turn and dried my tears.

◆ ◆ ◆

Summer camp turned out better than I had expected. In fact, it got to be fun after a while. But one night I woke up screaming with pain. I had a middle-ear infection. I was rushed to the hospital for an operation. Penicillin, which would have cured me, was still unknown at that time. I was very sick, and everybody thought I was going to die. After a long time, I got better, and the day came when Mama and Papa brought me home again. But Mama said she was not going to let me start school for another year. I didn't feel too good about that. By then I would be almost seven. Wouldn't the other children laugh at me?

But not going to school did not mean I could stay home and play with my dolls all day. I was introduced to gymnastics and, in winter, to skating lessons. Mama took me downtown for swimming classes in a public indoor pool. She wouldn't let me go there alone, because it meant going on the trolley. She said I was too young.

One day, on our weekly trip to downtown Stuttgart and the swimming pool, I saw several shops and office buildings draped with red, black, and white swastika flags. The swastika was the symbol of the Nazi party. The flags were nothing new to me. I had seen them before, on "special" occasions.

"Why are the flags flying today, Mama?" I asked.

"I suppose there's going to be another parade," she answered, and she started walking faster. I had to run to keep up with her. When we got to the pool, we found the other mamas and their daughters milling about outside.

"What is happening?" Mama asked one of the ladies.

In answer, her friend pointed to a sign stuck to the door with thumbtacks. Even though I wasn't going to school yet, I had no trouble spelling out the words:

JUDEN SIND UNERWÜNSCHT!

"Jews are not wanted," I read aloud, in case Mama and her friend hadn't read it correctly. "What does it mean?"

Mama's face was white. Her full, pink lips, which I always had thought so beautiful, all but disappeared. "It means . . . it means, Ollie, that we can't come here any more."

"No more swimming lessons?"

"No more swimming lessons for Jews."

◆ ◆ ◆

A month after my seventh birthday I entered first grade at a private girls' school. It was one of a few that still allowed Jewish children. In Germany, at that time, when a child's first school day arrived, she was given a large cone-shaped container made of brightly colored paper, which was filled with candies, chocolates, and cookies. I proudly carried mine to school, though it was almost as big as I was. All the other little girls had theirs.

My teacher's name was Fräulein Böhme. I loved her at once. Although I was older than most, I was still quite short for my age. I found this to be an advantage. At least no one was laughing at me. And soon I made new friends in my class. Brigitte had long, blond pigtails, and Hannele's hair was short and coal black. She and Marianne became my best friends. We walked together to school and back, and slept over at one another's houses. We moved from first to second to third grade together, and Fräulein Böhme remained our teacher throughout.

But one morning, when I was ten, a man in a dark suit came into our classroom and told us he was now our teacher. He wore a small red, white, and black badge in his lapel. In its center I saw a swastika.

"But where is Fräulein Böhme?" one girl asked.

"I am your teacher now," Herr Schüler repeated. "You will stand up when I speak to you and also when you speak to me. I expect you to raise your right arm in the Hitler salute. We will practice it now."

He raised his right arm straight ahead, his hand flat out, palm down, and loudly announced: "Heil Hitler!"

The other girls followed his example. "Heil Hitler!" they cried as loudly as they could. But not all of us saluted. Hannele and I, the only two Jewish children in the class, stiffly kept our arms to our sides. Only the day before Papa had told me that I didn't have to say it. I had been sitting on his lap in his favorite armchair while a voice on the radio next to us was screaming terrible things about Jews. Everything was the Jews' fault. "The Jews," claimed the voice, "are our undoing!" The voice, Papa told me, was Hitler's. He said the Nazis were holding a rally. The screaming voice went on and on, while thousands cheered. I felt like hiding somewhere. Even Piepsi, the canary, let out a shrill whistle. I think he was as scared as I. It was then that Papa said: "You don't ever have to say 'Heil Hitler.' "

But now I saw Herr Schüler's eyes on Hannele and me. If looks could kill, I thought. The next minute he thundered: "You two. Yes, you with the black hair. And you with the pink bow. Have you lost your tongues?"

I stood stock still and glared at my shoes, not daring to look up. Someone in back of the room snickered.

"I shall expect the Hitler salute from *every* girl in this room." He was still glowering at Hannele and me. "Is that understood? Now, once more. Heil Hitler!"

Without moving my head, I glanced to my side. To my surprise I saw Hannele's arm shoot straight out, palm down. Had she forgotten that she, too, was Jewish? My own arm felt like lead. I willed it to go halfway up, elbow bent. "Heil Hitler," I breathed through all but closed lips. Let him punish me, I thought, shaking with fear. He can't make me. Papa said I didn't have to.

But luckily, Herr Schüler grew tired of me. Perhaps he thought me too small or too stupid to bother with. We went on with our other lessons. At recess, in the school playyard, I found myself ignored by just about everybody, even Hannele. Even Marianne. Suddenly, I no longer had anyone to play with.

I told no one at home, though I think Frieda suspected that something was wrong.

"Don't dawdle so, Ollie," she said the next morning. "Finish your breakfast. You've hardly touched it. What's the matter? Don't you feel well? You'll be late for school if you don't—"

"I'm not hungry," I said. But she showed me no mercy. "Oh, all right." I forced another bite of bread and jam. But I couldn't swallow it. Pushing it into my cheek, I asked: "Please, can I go now?"

Instead of bouncing out of the house as usual, I dragged my feet and kept my hands in my pockets. My books and pencil box were inside my satchel strapped to my back. Today it felt heavy.

School was no longer fun, but it got no worse either. None of the girls wanted to play with me. Though Herr Schüler did not single me out again, he now ignored me all the time. I wasn't sure which was worse. If only Fräulein Böhme were back!

Then, in the middle of a night in November 1938, something happened that changed the course of history in the entire world. It also changed my life, forever.

4

KRISTALLNACHT

*N*ovember 9, 1938. Mama tucked me into my bed as usual and gave me a kiss. I wiped it off my cheek and tried to smile. But I couldn't help thinking about Frieda, as I had night and day since she had left. Was she back on her farm in Ochsenbach now? Did she miss me?

I missed her terribly. I had been told that her boyfriend had come to visit her in our house. There was nothing wrong with that, Mama said, but he was wearing his Nazi uniform. Naturally, my parents got upset about that. No one could be trusted anymore these days, Papa said, especially someone in uniform. In our house. And if he was Frieda's boyfriend, then maybe she couldn't be trusted either. Even though I found that last part really hard to believe, I could understand why they were afraid.

I never even had a chance to say good-bye to her. I'd cried myself to sleep every night since she left. I tried not to cry tonight, but it was no use. My tears started to roll down my cheeks, and I felt my pillow getting wet. Cook was gone, too. It seemed she didn't want to work for Jews anymore. Now Mama was doing all the cooking and house cleaning alone. I tried to help by dusting things and sweeping up the crumbs with a carpet cleaner after we'd eaten. I don't think I did too good a job, because I saw Mama going over everything again later.

Next I thought about Hans. He had been sent to school in England, so he wasn't here anymore either. When Papa was at work it was really quiet in our house. Mama must have felt so lonely with everybody gone, especially when I was in school. I tried looking at the bright side, the way Frieda would have. At least, I thought, in the evenings Mama and Papa and I still had each other. Even though I still felt as safe as a fairy princess in her castle, I knew I was really just an ordinary ten-year-old girl, going on eleven, to whom anything could happen. The castle walls didn't seem quite as strong anymore as I had imagined. I blew my nose and wiped my eyes. After a while I fell asleep.

A loud bang woke me. It must have been the middle of the night. I slid under my feather quilt to hide. Then I heard noisy footsteps stomping up the stairs. Right away I thought of the marching boots of Hitler's S.A. men, marching along the beautiful streets of downtown Stuttgart. Now I heard strange, gruff voices. Who was in our house? Why were they shouting? They seemed to be giving orders to someone. Doors banged. I thought I heard Mama crying softly. That scared me more than anything.

Was I dreaming? Another door banged. I stuffed the corner of my sheet into my mouth and didn't dare move. I barely breathed. I prayed the strange men in our house wouldn't find me. What was going on?

Suddenly everything was quiet once more. With just my eyes above the feather quilt, I watched as my door opened slowly. I held my breath. But no, it was not a strange man. It was only Mama tiptoeing into my room. I closed my eyes and started breathing again. I felt her cool hand on my head, but I pretended to be asleep. She sighed and left. A chink of light seeped through under my door. I listened a long time, but all remained quiet. I must have drifted off to sleep again.

◆ ◆ ◆

The first thing I noticed when I came downstairs for breakfast the next morning was that Mama's eyes were red, as if she had been crying. She looked as if she hadn't slept all night.

"Where is Papa?" I asked, expecting to see him at his usual place. His chair was empty.

"He . . . he's had to go away for a while." Mama's voice sounded strained, as if she'd been rehearsing a difficult line from a play. This whole time, since Hans and Frieda and Cook left, seemed unreal to me. Perhaps I *was* just having a bad dream, and any minute now I would wake up. Then I remembered the commotion in our house during the night. Had that been part of the dream, too?

Well, I thought, if she wants to play games, I'll play with her. I tried to act as if everything were perfectly normal. I stuffed my mouth with a large chunk of bread.

"When will he be back?" I knew I shouldn't talk with my mouth full. But Mama only shrugged and bent over her coffee cup. I frowned. Now I was certain that something terrible had happened. My hands grew cold. But I still tried to sound as if everything were normal.

"What shall I wear to school, Mama? I'll be late if I don't—"

Mama lifted her tired face: "You can't go to school today." Was I hearing her right? Or was this still part of my bad dream?

"Why not?"

"Because . . . you just can't."

"But if I don't go, Herr Schüler will—"

"You can't go there anymore. Soon you'll go to a new school. In a few days."

"What's wrong with the old one?" I cried in alarm. This was really becoming too much! But Mama had stopped listening. I watched her go to the telephone. She dialed and started yelling into the receiver. I heard her say Papa's name. Who was she talking to?

I tried to read, but all I did was turn pages without seeing them. I thought about how there were just the two of us, Mama and I. How crazy could it get? I wished that I would wake up *now*. That everything would be the way it was last year or even a month ago. . . . But it wasn't a dream, and I couldn't turn the clock back.

◆ ◆ ◆

When, some days later, Mama and I dared to take the trolley downtown, we couldn't believe our eyes. The Nazis had burned down the synagogue, leaving only a charred shell. All the other buildings on the same street were left unharmed. The windows of all the Jewish-owned shops had been smashed and the broken glass had been left all over the sidewalks. The next day everything had to be cleaned up, on Nazi orders. Who was made to do it? The Jewish store owners, we were told.

But they were no longer around. Papa was not the only one arrested that night. We learned that all men, from sixteen to sixty, were dragged out of their beds and taken away. Then who was left to clean up? Their wives and children, and the elderly. Or any Jew who was unlucky enough to be standing around at that place at that time.

Hitler came to Stuttgart not too long after that night— the night Papa disappeared. I wondered if the Führer wanted to see for himself what a good job his gangster storm troopers had done. On the day he came to town, Stuttgart was decked out with red, white, and black bunting and swastika flags, as if nothing had ever happened here.

Of course, we didn't have a flag. In fact, we Jews were not allowed to fly flags. Also, we were ordered not to come out of our houses during Hitler's parade. But I slipped out and went to see Frau Gumpel, next door. Frau Gumpel and her husband, Herr Gumpel, were our elderly neighbors. They had no children of their own, but they kept a toy chest in their house just for me.

I had forgotten to tell Mama where I was going. She went crazy looking for me. She was afraid the Nazis would do something to us if they found out I wasn't home. So she, too, disobeyed the order to stay in the house. She climbed over the fence, because she didn't want to be seen in the street, and found me at the Gumpels'. I could see on her face that she had trouble deciding whether to spank me or hug me. She hugged me!

◆ ◆ ◆

Since Papa was taken away Mama was on the phone morning, noon, and night. In her conversation, the name of a place kept coming up: *Dachau*. It was where Papa was. There was a concentration camp in this place. I had heard of concentration camps. They were prison camps where people who disagreed with Hitler were taken: communists, Gypsies, Roman Catholics, Jews, and others whom the Nazis didn't like. Stories were going around that prisoners there were being beaten up and tortured. I couldn't believe that anyone would want to beat up my Papa. Mama cried a lot, though she tried to hide it from me. I couldn't bear seeing her cry. It made me want to cry too.

◆ ◆ ◆

Up until that time I had no idea what being Jewish meant. We had never celebrated any of the Jewish holidays. Instead, we always had a Christmas tree, with real candles, and an egg hunt in our garden at Easter time. I was never inside the synagogue that had been burned the night the Nazis took Papa away. But about two weeks after that, I started going to a Jewish school.

The teacher told us that soon it would be Chanukah. Chanukah, she said, always comes near Christmastime. She said Jews shouldn't have Christmas trees. I told Mama about it and asked her if we could light Chanukah candles instead. I wanted to celebrate the festival of lights and freedom, as I had just learned. She took my hand without saying anything and lead me up to the third floor. In the storeroom, next to what used to be Frieda's room, were a lot of boxes filled with old letters, photographs, and Papa's medal from the Great War. Why had Mama brought me up here? I soon found out.

In a corner, behind all these boxes, we found a Chanukah *menorah*, a nine-branched candle holder. It was made of brass, quite small, and needed polishing. Mama let me carry it downstairs and we took turns rubbing it while I told her what I had learned about this holiday at my new school. The teacher had told us that Chanukah was about freedom, because Judah the Maccabee won his fight against the tyrant, Antiochus. To give thanks to God for his victory, he lit an oil lamp, and even though there was very little oil in it, it kept on burning for eight days. This night, when it started getting dark out, Mama and I lit the first candle and sang the songs that I had been given at school. They were all new to us, but we both loved them. I looked forward to the next seven nights, when another candle would be added to the first, until all eight would be blazing. I explained to her that the ninth branch, in the middle, was for the servant candle, the one used to light the others. We did not need a Christmas tree that year. But something was wrong.

"I wish Papa was here," I said, hugging Mama as hard as I could.

But Papa was still in the Dachau concentration camp. At least Hans was safe in England by now, or he would have been taken there too. The Stuttgart synagogue was not the only one burned down. As we learned later, almost all synagogues, in all Germany, were burnt to the ground. There was so much broken glass lying in the streets that it was hard to walk about. That is why that night was later called *Kristallnacht*, Crystal Night. The Night of Broken Glass.

◆ ◆ ◆

One day, as I was walking home from my new Jewish school, I saw Marianne come toward me. My best friend. I was so glad to see her. I wanted to ask her if anybody missed me and if Herr Schüler ever said anything about my absence. But before I could wave to her, she crossed the street. I couldn't believe it! I knew she had seen me, because she had started to wave to me. Then, suddenly, her hand still only halfway up, she crossed the street. She just kept on walking, without even turning her head, as if she never knew me at all.

I felt angry and confused. I ran the rest of the way home, crying all the way.

"She was afraid," Mama tried to explain to me.

"Of me? I'm her best friend!"

"Her parents must have told her not to speak to you anymore."

"But, why?"

"Because Aryans are not allowed to talk to Jews now."

"What's Aryan?"

"That is what Hitler calls anyone who is German."

"But we are German!"

"Yes, I know." I knew Mama was trying to sound patient. "But we are also Jewish."

"That doesn't make any sense!" I yelled. "I wish Papa would come home!"

◆ ◆ ◆

On December 28, my birthday, Papa came back. He came home in the middle of the night, while I was sleeping. It had been the middle of night when the Nazis had come for him, six long weeks ago. This time, Mama woke me. I hugged Papa and never wanted to let him go. But

I saw how he had changed. He was too thin, and he didn't have much hair left. He didn't smile. I wondered if his eyes were looking at the terrible things that must have happened in that ghastly place, Dachau. I wanted to ask him: Did they really beat you up? But before I could, he said he couldn't talk about anything. They told him they'd come and get him again if he did. I wondered, though, if he ever told Mama.

Papa never went back to his office again. The Nazis "bought" the publishing company, which in reality meant they stole it. Papa brought his rolltop desk and a few other items home and set up an office in the playroom on the third floor. From there he did some work every day, though I never really understood what it was he did. I loved having him home all the time. I also loved the smell of his cigar, which now permeated the playroom— I mean, office. Poor Mama. She couldn't stand the smell.

This year was the first that I didn't have a birthday party. I remembered another birthday, a long time ago, when our neighbor, Herr Kopfer, came over and did some magic tricks for me and my friends. And three years ago, on my eighth, Cook baked a special cake for me in the shape of the number 8. For this birthday, my eleventh, there was no party. But I did get my usual four-leaf clover pot. As always, it had a little red wooden mushroom hidden in it, for good luck. I thought we could all use some good luck right now.

◆ ◆ ◆

While Papa was still in Dachau, Mama decided that it would be best that I go to England for a while. She had heard about something called *Kindertransport,* Children's Transport. This was a system planned by the Jewish Refugee Committee to transport Jewish children to England, away from the growing danger in Germany. In England they would live in safety with English families. Already, trains filled with children were leaving every day. Mama had my name put on the list, and now we were waiting for my turn to come up. It could happen any day. In the meantime, Mama started packing things. Other preparations for my leaving began, that made me realize the seriousness of it all.

In January 1939, a man started coming to the house to teach me English. His name was Mr. Cooperson. Mr. Cooperson was bony and had greasy hair. I hated him. But I learned to say "The dog is under the table" in English. I didn't learn much else, and I certainly did not want to go to England. Why couldn't I stay in Stuttgart with Mama and Papa? I remembered summer camp. I had fallen sick there, but I had come home. This would not be the same at all. What if I never came back from England?

◆ ◆ ◆

At school we learned about Purim, the next Jewish holiday to come up. Teacher told us about the wicked Haman. Haman, prime minister of Persia thousands of years ago, had planned to kill all the Jews in his country. But Queen Esther heard about it and told her husband, King Ahasuerus, and Haman was hanged.

That evening, when Mama kissed me good night, I said: "I think the wicked Haman was just like the wicked Hitler." Mama turned pale and told me not to say such things. "The walls have ears," she said. I imagined little ears all over the blue walls of my room and giggled. Still, I thought, I'd better not say such things anymore. I knew what she meant. You never knew *who* might be listening!

Soon after Purim, a letter came from the Refugee Committee, saying that I was to leave on March 3. That was a month away. A week later, I got sick. My head hurt. I threw up my breakfast. Mama took my temperature and said I had a fever. She called Dr. Oppenheimer. He came over, walked into my room, took one look at me and said: "Measles." I secretly hoped this would postpone my departure.

Even while I was ill, our seamstress came to the house to sew new clothes for me. I liked the school uniforms she was making for me. Mrs. Liebman, the lady the committee said I was to stay with, had sent us a drawing of one. All the school girls in England wore them, she wrote. I thought I looked quite good in mine, except that my legs were too skinny.

Mama was busy packing all my stuff in crates and suit-cases. An S.A. man in brown Nazi uniform came and stood around, watching her. I didn't know why he was there, because all he did was get in Mama's way. When it came to my cello, he asked if this was something valu-able. Mama knew I would not be allowed to take any-thing of value along. So she laughed and said: "This old thing?" Luckily, he didn't know that, sometimes, the older a musical instrument is, the more valuable it becomes. The cello came with me, but, as it turned out, I didn't see it again for a long time. Mama even packed Peter, my favorite doll, although I told her I didn't think I would have much use for him in England. Did she want every-body to think I was a baby? She packed the doll anyway.

Another letter came from the Liebmans in England. There was a color-tinted photograph in it of the family. Their daughter seemed to be about my age. The pastel colors made them look funny, and their lips were too red. I asked Mama, what if they don't like me? "Of course they will like you," she said.

Even if they do, I thought, I won't like them.

◆ ◆ ◆

March 3, 1939. Before I knew it, the fateful day ar-rived. There was no stopping it. I still had a few spots from the measles, but the doctor said I was no longer contagious. This was the day I was to go to England! I was excited and fearful all at the same time. Here I was, eleven years old, and leaving home all by myself. It was hard to separate the two emotions. One minute I wanted to laugh, the next to cry. To overcome my confusion, I talked. Nonstop.

Mama got permission to go with me on the train as far as Wiesbaden, where her mother, my Oma, lived. I had said good-bye yesterday to Herr and Frau Gumpel. They said they wished they could come too. But the train was only for children. I hoped that they would be able to leave Germany soon, too. They looked so sad.

Mama said that she and Papa thought they would get to England in about six weeks, "God willing." The way she said it, I was not sure whether I believed her. A thought kept coming into my head: What if we never see each other again? I tried not to think about this.

Before we left for the station, I walked from room to room, starting upstairs and all the way into the cellar where the wine was kept, and where the laundry was done. I wanted to remember every corner forever. Piepsi, the canary, was perched in his cage under the rubber tree, which by now had reached to the ceiling. The little bird cocked his yellow head and looked at me with his bright, shiny eyes, but he didn't sing. I was sure he knew I was leaving.

Herr Kopfer, our neighbor the magician, drove Mama, Papa, and me to the station. We thought we were early, but when we got there, some children were already on the train. I kissed and hugged Papa hard. He tried to smile, but something funny was happening to his mouth. I hugged him again, so he wouldn't see my scrunched up face. He and the other fathers did not have permission from the Nazis to come into the train. We all tried so hard to be brave.

Mama and I climbed aboard. I waved to Papa until he was only a tiny speck in the distance. The train turned a curve, and he was gone.

An hour or so later we pulled into Wiesbaden. I pressed my face against the window to look for Oma. I had been here many times before. But today I could not get off the train. Instead, Oma came to the train to say good-bye to me. I saw her round, sweet face, anxiously peering into each car before we had even come to a full stop. Mama stood up suddenly, gave me another kiss and said: "Remember to be a good girl." Then she quickly jumped off the train. The platform teemed with people of all ages. Many wore Nazi uniforms. The train filled up with more children. Their parents stood under the train windows, looking forlorn. Some were crying. The children were excited. Some cried too, others were silent, with their lips pressed together. The hands of the big station clock under the steamed-up glass dome moved on relentlessly. The station master shouted: "*Alles einsteigen!*" "All aboard!" and slowly we started to move again. I leaned out as far as I could. Other children behind me pushed and shoved to get a last glimpse as well. While we were still moving slowly, Oma reached up and slipped a small package into my hand. There wasn't even time to say thank you as the train began to gather speed. I slipped Oma's gift into my coat pocket, waving with my other hand until I couldn't see Mama or Oma anymore. Tears were streaming down my face.

Now the steam engine had gathered full speed. Soon I saw that we had left the city and were hurling through the countryside. I suddenly needed to go to the bathroom. When I came back out, some children were laughing and pointing at me. I looked down and saw that my blue wool-knit dress was tucked into my matching underpants. I was furious—perhaps at them, perhaps at myself, perhaps at this whole situation. Quickly I fixed my clothes and sat stiffly in my seat. I had to keep rubbing my wet eyes.

5

JOURNEY TO ENGLAND

The train rushed past pine woods, shimmering lakes, rivers, and distant mountains, past towns and villages and church spires like spears poking holes in the gray sky. After some hours, the landscape became even flatter. Raindrops splashed against the windows and ran down in rivulets, making crazy patterns from top to bottom. The train slowed down. We were at the Dutch border.

This time there was no Papa to take care of passports. I was one of about a hundred children, from about four years old to seventeen. We were supervised by a few adults from the Jewish Refugee Committee, who carried our papers. German officers came strutting through our compartments. They checked us off on their lists. In their black uniforms; red, white, and black swastika armbands; high-peaked caps; and especially tall, polished boots, they looked menacing. One or two stopped to ask some of the children a question. To me they sounded like snarling dogs. I slouched into my seat, hoping they wouldn't notice me. As they passed me, one man looked at me and was about to speak. But his comrade pushed him from behind, pointing at his watch. They kept going.

With a shudder the train moved forward a few yards and stopped again. Some children had been standing. They tumbled over. Now it was the turn of the Dutch customs officials. These men had smiles on their faces, and although we couldn't understand a word they said, we knew they were saying "Welcome to Holland." We all relaxed. Even the little ones stopped crying. Every now and then my fingers touched Oma's last-minute present, still stuffed into my pocket. Soon, I promised myself, I would open it.

After a little while longer, we were allowed off the train. Down we spilled onto the platform, where the Dutch women were waiting for us. They gave us hot cocoa and cookies. They, too, had smiles on their faces.

But all too soon we were herded into a large room to wait for the ship. The Dutch harbor, Hoek van Holland, lies on the English Channel, directly across from a town in England called Harwich. The sea in the Channel is famous for its stormy winds and swelling waves. This night was typical.

With the cocoa and cookies swishing about in my stomach, I bravely boarded the ship. I was shown my cabin, which I was to share with another girl. She was older than I—maybe sixteen or seventeen. Up to now I had kept my feelings bottled up inside. Being by nature a quiet child, I had said very little. But now, when I heard my cabin mate cry in her bed, I too began to feel a lump in my throat. I buried my head into my pillow, clenched my fists in fear and anger, and wept. To make matters worse, I began to feel seasick. Our little ship was tossed about on the fierce sea, heaving and yawing, and with it my stomach. Eventually, exhaustion forced us both into a few hours of restless sleep.

By daybreak we steamed into the harbor of Harwich. All was calm. Most of the people of that small fishing town were still asleep. I wondered how many knew that a boatload of very young refugees from Hitler's Germany had just arrived on their shores? But a few were there to greet us. They spoke yet another language, which we did not understand.

I soon realized that my newly acquired phrase, "The dog is under the table," would be of no use to me in this situation. By chance, my fingers touched something in my pocket. It was Oma's present. I pulled out the little package and tore the paper off. Here were two tiny books, one blue, the other red. Each was so little, it could easily fit into the palm of my hand. These books were to prove my most valuable possessions in the next few months to come. They were dictionaries: one German to English, the other English to German.

In the beginning, these little friends were with me

always. If I didn't understand what was being said to me—which was most of the time—out would come my little red companion: English to German. I would simply hand it over to the speaker, who would show me the word. Then I would fish in my pocket for the blue one and find the reply in German. I would try to pronounce its English equivalent, which sometimes convulsed us both into laughter.

Anyway, for now I didn't have to rely on the spoken word in order to understand. I was marched off with the rest to the nearby Harwich station and put on a train to London, the capital city of England. I usually liked train rides. But by now I had really had enough. I must have been so tired that morning that I slept all the way. That's why I did not see the gently rolling hills of the English countryside, covered with fields and woods. I slept past the farmhouses, or "cottages." To this day, many have roofs covered by straw, or "thatch." Often the thatch-work is done in lovely patterns. It keeps the houses cool in summer, warm in winter, and sheds the rainwater. There is always a chimney or two, since many English houses rely, even today, on fireplaces for heat. Smoke would have been coming out of the chimneys as we raced by. I slept.

Horses, cows, pigs, chickens, children on their way to school, farmers going to work in their fields—all must have looked up when our train swished by. People leaning on their bicycles would have waited patiently, as they do today, at the lowered cross guards. *Ratattat, ratattat, ratattat, tooooot!* Still I slept.

When we finally stopped, I rubbed my eyes. Where was I? Mama? Papa? Then I remembered. This must be London. I must look out for Hans. He was supposed to meet me here.

6

LYDIA

*T*here he was! I quickly spotted his red hair in the crowd. When had he become a man? I counted quickly on my fingers. He was eighteen now.

Hans patted me on the head—brothers and sisters don't kiss—and grabbed my bag. I skipped after him into the Underground—the London subway system. My numbered cardboard tag, which I was still wearing from the *Kindertransport*, bounced from a string around my neck. We got off the Underground within walking distance of his place.

Hans lived in a rented room. His landlady was waiting at the door to greet us. Her daughter, who looked a little older than I, was at her side. A white terrier dog ran up to me. I backed up, not sure whether he wanted to play or take a nip out of my leg.

"Don't worry. His name is Spot. He's very friendly," the girl said. I *thought* it was what she said, for I didn't understand the words at all. Like Spot, I only got the meaning of her words from her tone of voice. The older woman took a picture of us with the Brownie box camera I brought along. It used to belong to Mama. She had given it to me . . . yesterday. Was that only yesterday? I swallowed a lump and forced myself to think: Now I can say "the dog is under the table."

"Tonight you'll sleep here," Hans told me. "Then tomorrow I'll go with you to the Liebmans. My boss gave me the day off."

"Boss? Don't you go to school anymore?" I asked. It seemed, in all the excitement of the last few weeks, no one had bothered to tell me anything.

"No. I need to earn some money now, you see. I work in a radio factory. Our parents have enough problems of their own right now."

I hung my head. At the mention of Mama and Papa, that silly lump formed in my throat again. Once again, I swallowed it. "I know," I agreed. Then, as if to cheer him up, I said: "I remember when you were home, you always fiddled around with radios and stuff. Remember the telephone? Two tin cans on a string? You went in one room, I in another. The string was supposed to carry the sound of our voices, like telephone wires."

He chuckled. "I remember. To tell you the truth, we could have just shouted to one another."

"Yes. But it was fun."

For a minute I forgot the reality of the moment. Then it hit me again. I am not at home with Mama and Papa. Mama is not about to call us for lunch. Tonight I will sleep in a strange bed—and all the nights to follow, maybe for six whole weeks. Or even longer.

Mrs. Williams, the landlady, must have sensed what I was thinking. She put her arm around me and led me into her house.

"Come on, then, love. Let's have some tea and biscuits, shall we? You'll feel better with something inside you."

This was how I first found out about tea and biscuits. "Biscuits" is what the English call cookies. Tea and biscuits are the national remedy for whatever ails you. In England, as I was soon to learn, we had tea and biscuits between breakfast and lunch and between lunch and supper. It slows down the pace and lets you catch your breath. Even now I wonder why everyone in the world doesn't have the custom of tea and biscuits.

That afternoon, Hans and I sent a telegram to Mama and Papa to tell them I had arrived.

◆　◆　◆

On my second day in England, I was taken to my new family, the Liebmans. They lived in a poor section of London. It meant another train ride on the Underground. By now I was thoroughly sick of trains. I wouldn't care if I never saw another train in my whole life! When we got there, all the houses looked alike. But Hans and I found the street and the right number, and we

climbed down a few steps from the sidewalk to the front
door. It needed painting. In a tiny patch of earth in front
of it, a faded rose struggled bravely to stay alive.

Hans set down my suitcase and rang the bell. I adjusted
my navy blue cap and pulled at my tan coat. My dress,
the one with the matching underpants, felt scratchy. My
heart was racing a hundred miles a second. Stuttgart was
so very far away.

Scuffling footsteps. The door was flung open. But I could
see nothing. It was dismally dark inside, much darker than
the cloudy day outside. Out of the darkness, a woman in
a cotton house dress appeared. Her bare feet were stuck
in floppy old slippers. They were not like the slippers
Mama kept in our vestibule to keep the white linoleum
from scuff marks. These looked . . . well . . . they looked
like a couple of moth-eaten rats. A girl crept up behind
her. She was thin like me, but at least a head taller. She
wore a bathrobe with brown stains on it. The robe might
have been pink once.

"Is that her, Mum?" the girl seemed to be asking,
pointing at me. To which the girl's mother seemed to be
saying: "Shush, Lydia, that's rude."

Mrs. Liebman, Lydia's "mum," asked us in. I tried to
follow her words. I thought she was apologizing to Hans
about the state of her apartment. She might have said
something like: "It isn't much, but it's home." Then she
said the two words that I got to learn very early on:

"Some tea?" Her tired eyes avoided mine. The girl, Lydia, stood awkwardly rooted to the floor, gawking at me and scratching her head.

"Lydia, what's got into you? Get a move on and put the kettle up, there's the girl!" her mother said. Or something like that.

Lydia gave me another long, scathing look and ran to do what her mum told her to do.

Hans seemed ill at ease. He gulped his tea and said "no thanks" to seconds.

"Have to get back to work," he muttered, thoughtfully translating this into German for me. I knew perfectly well that his boss had given him the day off, but I didn't say anything. He jumped off the sagging sofa, making the springs snap back, and shook Mrs. Liebman's hand. Nodding to Lydia and me, he headed for the door. I ran after him. He pummelled my back. I took it to mean: "Chin up, kiddo. It could be worse!" Then he was gone.

I was on my own.

◆　◆　◆

There wasn't much to the house. The front room, where we had our tea, was used only for "company." It was small and crowded with seldom-used, overstuffed furniture that was usually covered with sheets. A small glass-front cabinet held a few china cups and saucers. A vase filled with paper flowers stood in the fireplace. There were no bookshelves, no books.

In back, the room used as the family room was actually the kitchen. It was as dark as everything else and had a sickening smell of stale coffee and raw onions. I tried not to think about Cook's wonderful odors from our kitchen back home. In a corner was a large birdcage. But instead of Piepsi the canary, its occupant was Polly, a green parrot. He regarded me with sad, beady eyes, then turned his attention to adjusting his bedraggled feathers. "Polly want a cracker?" was to become my second English phrase, after "the dog is under the table."

"Show her the bedroom, Lydia," Mrs. Liebman said. She hadn't called me by my name yet.

Sulking, Lydia led me to the bedroom, next to the kitchen. A tiny window over our heads let in whatever light came in from the street above. I could see people's feet as they walked past it, to and fro. By now it had started to rain, and the feet splashed drops of water and mud onto the tiny windowpane.

"This is mine," Lydia said, pointing to the bed on our left. The sheets and blankets were rumpled up, and the pillow squashed into a ball. A cat slept on top of it all. Mama would have been horrified. I stroked the cat.

"What she is called?"

For the first time, Lydia giggled. "Mittens. And this is yours. Mum hasn't had time to put your sheets on yet." I flopped onto the unmade bed, shoes and all, and didn't move for two hours!

Little by little I adjusted to my new life. Mrs. Liebman

was always tired. She sighed a great deal and ordered
Lydia around a lot. Me she more or less ignored. Mr.
Liebman was seen only on weekends. He had a night job
and slept during the day. I never got to see the master
bedroom. He kept the door closed all the time. On Friday
nights he had dinner with us. Mrs. Liebman lit Shabbat
candles, and Mr. Liebman said the blessings over the bread
and wine. On Saturday mornings he went to synagogue.
When he came home, we all ate together. After that, he
would sit in a lumpy old armchair in the kitchen, read
the papers, and drink beer. Sunday afternoons he went to
bed, and by Sunday night he was back at work.

Our bedroom had a washstand with a porcelain bowl
and pitcher. The toilet was outdoors, behind the kitchen.
This being only March, it was cold out there, and smelly.
In order to flush, you had to pull on a chain. Sometimes
it worked, sometimes it didn't.

As for Lydia, she's part of the story I would like to
forget.

Lydia teased me without mercy. She would give me
something, then snatch it away. Steal my socks, my hair
brush, the food off my plate. Pinch my arm when nobody
was looking, then stare me down, waiting for me to cry.
I never did. She'd say something to me very fast, then
laugh with glee at my expression. She knew I hadn't
understood a word. If I said something to her in German,
she would simply skip away, her nose in the air.

At the time, I was too engrossed in my own miseries

to understand why she behaved this way. Only now, many years later, does it occur to me that Lydia must have been bewildered, as was I, and certainly jealous. I can imagine that she might have thought: "Who is this scrawny looking brat whom my mum makes me share my room with? And she doesn't even speak English?" Perhaps her parents had tried to explain to her before my arrival about the dangers of Jewish life in Germany. Perhaps they had all decided as a family that, because they themselves were Jewish, they would take in one little Jewish girl in order that she might escape. Perhaps. Or perhaps not. I realize now that in the Liebman family there was very little communication. Lydia could not have understood what was going on. As I could not.

And yet, I think, in time I would have adjusted to my new life with the Liebmans, and with Lydia, if it hadn't been for the endless scratching.

◆ ◆ ◆

From the first I noticed Lydia scratching her head all the time. I thought it was a habit she had. But soon my own scalp began to itch. After a while I was scratching just as she was. In the mornings, when I woke up, in what little light there was, I could see tiny blood stains on my pillow. What awful disease had I caught from this girl?

Mrs. Liebman made me sit down every Saturday to answer my parents' letters, which came regularly once a week. They were always short and cheerful and didn't tell me anything that I really wanted to know. If everything was so fine, I wondered, then why was I here in England? I kept my masterpieces short, too. After all, I thought, why upset my parents? To make the letters look longer, I filled empty spaces with little drawings. Thus parrots and cats marched across the printed lines, as did clever portraits of me with the family Liebman. I did not enjoy writing letters, so I filled up the pages as quickly as possible with whatever came to mind. One particular letter must have mentioned the fact that my head was itching. Mama must have received this information with some dismay. She went into action immediately, for not long after, I had a visitor.

"Someone to see you, love," announced Mrs. Liebman. I was in the kitchen, trying to teach Polly the parrot some German.

"Me?" Who would come to see me? Who even knew I existed? I scratched my head and rushed to the front room, where all visitors were received.

My guest sat stiffly on the edge of one of the overstuffed chairs, from which the sheets had been removed. Her hat was of the very latest style. It partly covered her face. I judged her to be about thirty-five or forty. She smelled wonderfully of health and cleanliness, with just a touch of some heavenly perfume. Her blond hair was neatly combed back and caught in a bun at the nape of her neck. Even my untrained eyes could see that the suit she wore was well-tailored and no doubt very expensive. She wore silk stockings, with seams straight up the middle of her legs, and high-heeled shoes that matched her suit. She looked vaguely familiar.

Before I plopped myself in the chair across from hers, she held out a gloved hand to me.

"My name is Mrs. Gordon. My husband and I came to visit your parents in Stuttgart last year, on business. You may not remember."

So that's where I had seen her before!

"How do you do?" I said in my budding English.

She smiled.

"Very well, thank you. I have a little girl at home, just about your age. How would you like to come and stay with us?"

I thought it over.

"You mean for the weekend sometime?" I asked.

"No, I mean live with us." She coughed into her gloved hand. "Until a more permanent place can be found for you."

I hadn't the slightest idea what "permanent" meant. All I heard was "live with us."

"But what about Mrs. Liebman?" I asked, not knowing what else to say.

"Don't worry. I've already spoken to her. She will have you ready by Monday morning."

So everything had already been arranged. Asking me

was only a formality. Though, truthfully, after four weeks of Lydia I was more than willing to leave. Besides, in only two more weeks the six weeks would be up. Mama and Papa would be here then!

How could I have known that Mrs. Gordon's little girl was to prove a far worse headache than Lydia had ever been?

7

JILL

*T*hat weekend I spent with my head in the kitchen sink, while Mrs. Liebman scrubbed my scalp as if her life depended upon it. I feared that I would have no skin left on my head, let alone hair. The soap she used reeked. I wanted to throw up. I protested loudly. But the more I screamed, the harder she scrubbed.

Lydia was noticeably absent.

"Never mind Lydia. Her turn is coming. She can't get away with it this time," her mother snarled. I lifted my head to rub some stinky soap out of my burning eyes. "Not yet! I'm not done with you, young lady! There will not be a single louse left on you when you go to your new place, if I have anything to do with it." With that she scrubbed harder than before. I felt as if somehow the whole business had been my fault.

But I had recognized a word: *louse*. In German the word sounds the same: *Laus*. Now I knew what I had caught from Lydia. I was mortified. I lowered my head

obediently into the smelly sink and let Mrs. Liebman
scrub away.

◆ ◆ ◆

On Monday morning a shiny black limousine parked
outside the dreary basement flat of the Liebmans'. I
watched from behind the sooty lace curtains as a chauffeur opened the car door. A slender leg in silk stockings
and high-heeled shoes emerged. Mrs. Gordon had come
to fetch me.

My head still felt sore from the delousing. But at least
it didn't itch anymore. Mr. Liebman was already sleeping.
Mrs. Liebman, much to my surprise, kissed me on the
cheek. Lydia pinched my arm one last time. I quickly
stepped on her foot. Then I was off and away.

Through the limousine windows I watched London fly
past us. Cathedrals. Department stores. People rushing
about. Women with umbrellas and shopping bags over
their arms. Men swinging umbrellas and briefcases. Little
dogs straining on leashes, as little dogs will. Lines of children snaking along in twos, a teacher in front and one in
back to catch the stragglers. Suddenly I thought of my
real school in Stuttgart, and even of Herr Schüler. A huge
wave of homesickness threatened to drown me.

I was very quiet. After some time we left the busy city
behind. After more than two hours' drive through the
English countryside, we came to another city.

"Norwich," explained Mrs. Gordon. It was the first thing she had said since we had left London.

More old buildings, black with age. A cathedral. People rushing about. Children. Dogs. My breath was steaming up the windowpanes, as we hurriedly drove past.

Soon we came to the suburbs. Wrought-iron fences and tall hedges hid the houses behind them. At first they were quite small, semidetached and all alike. Gradually they became larger, more opulent. At times they could barely be seen from the road. They stood, like palaces, at the end of long, tree-lined driveways. Tall, graceful Elizabethan chimneys emitted smoke, the only sign that people lived there.

Our limousine turned into one such driveway and pulled up to the entrance of what looked to me like a castle. The chauffeur came around to open the door for Mrs. Gordon and me.

No sooner was I out of the car than a girl about my size hurled herself out of the house and threw herself at her mother.

"Mummie! Mummie! Where were you so long? I wanted to come with you! And we have to get to the stables by half past two, have you forgotten?"

I was beginning to recognize one or two words here and there, but she was certainly speaking much too fast. All I got was: "Mummie," "Come with you," and "half past two." I checked my watch. It was only eleven.

Her mother said something reassuring to her, dismissed the chauffeur, and led the way inside.

My eyes nearly popped out of my head. The cool, marbled foyer was filled with great pots of flowers. At home, Mama also kept flowers in the house, but only in summertime. I had never heard of flowers before May, at the earliest. This was only April. Where had they come from? I learned later that in back of the garden were greenhouses, where gardeners coaxed flowers and tropical plants to grow all year round. But I didn't know that then. I was very impressed.

Again I had to share a room, this time with soft, frilly beds, neatly made up. I wondered briefly what Mama was using my blue room for these days. This room was all pink and white. Blue, I thought, would have been better.

The girl's name was Jill. She was quite pretty. Her long yellow curls fell softly about her shoulders. She had a way of tossing her head when she spoke that made them dance as if they had a life of their own. Her eyes were as blue as mine. But I had this creepy feeling that evil lurked behind them. Evil? Well, perhaps just . . . hate. Just looking at them made me shiver. She wore Shirley Temple shoes. Patent leather. Black. I looked down at my own sturdy oxfords. Laced. Brown. I wished I could hide my feet under the plush carpet.

We had tea in a glassed-in breakfast room that led into the garden. I tried to follow the conversation, but no luck. Jill was obviously talking about me. She pointed at me several times and giggled maliciously. But from Mrs. Gordon's voice I could tell that she told Jill to stop it. Jill stuck out her tongue at me, then pouted.

Lunch was served an hour later in the formal dining room. A fire roared in the fireplace. If it hadn't been for Jill, everything would have been perfect.

Mrs. Gordon spoke to me in German. It sounded funny, and I was dying to laugh at the way she pronounced the words. But in my head I could hear Mama telling me to be polite. Mrs. Gordon said I could come along to watch Jill have her riding lessons.

The girl changed into her riding clothes. She left her frilly white dress rumpled on her bed, jumped into her jodhpurs, and pulled up her wondrous boots. Oh, to have an outfit like that, I thought. Then, with her helmet under her arm, she stepped into the waiting car, ahead of her mother. I followed slowly, kicking pebbles along the driveway. The chauffeur drove us to the stables.

Jill pranced merrily around the field on a fine-looking mare, while Mrs. Gordon and I perched on the rail, watching her. For the first time in all my eleven years, I knew what envy was. To wear those riding clothes—that would have been one thing. But to sit proudly atop a sleek, muscular animal such as this horse—oh, that would have been paradise itself! Its long, blond mane flowed in the wind; its gentle eyes grew wild with excitement as its hoofs, barely touching the ground, thundered past. Oh, I wanted to ride! I became obsessed by the thought. I would learn English quickly, so that I could tell Mrs. Gordon that I wanted to ride.

But when I learned enough to ask, the answer was always the same: "Soon. Maybe next time. Yes, soon."

Days melted into weeks, weeks into yet another month. On Sundays, Jill went to church with her parents, while I stayed home with the housekeeper. On Mondays and Thursdays I was taken along to Jill's riding lessons. Always I hoped that this time my prayers would be answered.

They never were. Was Mrs. Gordon so insensitive? Or was she simply unaware that this strange little creature, me—whom she surely had rescued from a life of poverty in the slums of London, and from certain persecution, possibly death, in Germany—could think of wanting any-thing more?

In Stuttgart I had been the spoiled darling of my fam-ily. All I had to do was ask, and sooner or later I'd get what I wanted. I thought of the longed-for scooter, and the roller skates, now unused and rusting in back of some closet at home. Now I was the onlooker; Jill the spoiled darling. I . . . I was merely the guest passing through, until a "more permanent" home could be found for me. For I knew that Mrs. Gordon had no intentions of keep-ing me. Whatever would she do with this little Jewish refugee?

I began to fight with Jill.

I fought for what I had come to expect from the world. I fought for what I thought were my rights. I used my feet, my hands, my fingernails. I changed from being an easy-to-please, cheerful child into a screaming, snarling, scratching, spitting little monster. The world, as it turned out, didn't care. But Mrs. Gordon did.

"If you don't behave yourself," she told me, "I will have to send you back to Germany."

8

BOARDING SCHOOL

Well, of course, that didn't happen. Though, as you might imagine, I had mixed feelings about her threat. Back to Germany? Back to Mama and Papa? What could be so bad? By now the six originally promised weeks had turned into several months. Why did I have to be here anyway? Had anybody ever asked me?

But I wasn't totally stupid. I knew. I knew that I was better off here, no matter how awful I might think it. It was still better here than back home in Germany, where unspeakable things were happening to Jews. I knew that if Mama and Papa didn't manage to leave soon, Papa might wind up in Dachau again. Or worse! The reason they had let him out in the first place was that they made him promise to leave Germany. I knew my parents were trying in every way possible to leave. They wouldn't give up; I knew that. The question was mainly: Where to? They had sent me here to England, where Hans had come before me, where we both would be safe, where life was still normal, and where no one hated another for having a different religion. I couldn't let them down. I was sure they wouldn't be too pleased to see me back.

For two whole days I managed not to fight with Jill. It was hard. I felt the pressure building up inside me, like a tea kettle with water boiling inside and no place to let it out. Tomorrow was another riding lesson. Maybe this time . . .

But there was to be no "this time." Soon after break-fast that day, I had yet another visitor. She was small, quite frail, her white hair combed back tightly from her face and coiled on top of her head. She wore steel-rimmed glasses and old-fashioned, clean, sensible clothes. She looked extremely old to me, though she probably wasn't much over sixty. Her cheeks were rosy pink.

"Say how d'you do to Miss Carter," Mrs. Gordon told me. "She's the headmistress of the boarding school for girls in Norwich." She told me its name. "Miss Carter has very kindly agreed to take you on."

Miss Carter took off her brown leather gloves and of-fered me her hand. I shook it politely and curtsied, as Mama had always expected of me. My tongue was stuck to the roof of my mouth.

"I expect you will like it very much at my school," said Miss Carter in a tinkly voice like a silver bell. She smiled kindly, and I could hear her false teeth click in her mouth. "We're all very excited about your coming."

I had a million questions, but they all got glued to the back of my throat.

As a last well-meaning gesture, Mrs. Gordon's chauffeur was ordered to take us to the boarding school. As I looked back I saw Jill waving to me. She was wearing her riding outfit.

◆   ◆   ◆

"What's your name?"

"How old are you?"

"Where d'you come from?"

"Don't you speak English?"

The girls clustered around me, all talking at once. They sounded like sparrows twittering. Here and there I recognized a word or two.

"No English. German," I said.

"Sprechen Sie Deutsch?" said one, a heavy girl with thick glasses and long hair. The others were convulsed in laughter. I was the only one who didn't get the joke. With her atrocious pronunciation I had not even understood the question!

We were gathered in the courtyard of the old mansion that served as the boarding school. It was situated on a pleasant, tree-lined street on the outskirts of the city. The tall steeple of the famous cathedral could be seen above the rooftops, if you twisted your head just so.

All the girls wore uniforms. They looked so smart in their mauve tunics over lilac blouses and purple blazers.

Their school ties were purple, black, and white striped, knotted just like a boy's. They all had on black velour hats with hatbands that were striped the same colors as the ties.

Instantly, my yearning to ride a horse was replaced for such a uniform. The tunic that Mama had our seamstress make for me before I left Stuttgart was close, but not quite right. For one thing, it was navy blue, not mauve. Also, the pleats were altogether different. I longed to look like everybody else.

An older girl approached our little cluster. She was about fifteen, maybe sixteen.

"Sh! Here comes June!" someone whispered. They flew apart like a flock of birds at the fall of her footsteps. To my surprise, June headed straight for me.

She held out her hand and smiled. She wore the same blazer as everyone else, but on her lapel I noticed a little pin in the shape of a capital *P*. That must stand for something important, I thought.

"I'm June," she said. Rudely I stared at her pin. "Oh," she laughed, "that means I'm a prefect. Sort of puts me in charge of the younger girls, like you. First you get to be a junior prefect, then a prefect. Do you want to come with me to my dormitory? I think I have an old uniform up there that I outgrew. It might fit you. If not, we'll make it fit. Won't hurt trying it on, anyway."

I understood "come with me," and "uniform." The rest didn't really matter.

Oh, if all my wishes could have been fulfilled as quickly as this one! From that day on, I stuck close to June. I found out that she was Miss Carter's niece. Not only was she a prefect, she was the head prefect. Her power was absolute.

The girls my age began to tease me. "June's little pet," they called me when they thought I couldn't hear or that I didn't understand. But I was learning the language faster than they realized. I decided it might be better to stop trailing June.

◆ ◆ ◆

We had a French teacher that everybody hated. Her name was Mademoiselle Donaldson. It didn't sound so French to me. I think I hated her more than the other girls did, though. After all, I thought, I had enough to do to cope with English, never mind French! I enthusiastically helped set a trap for Mademoiselle Donaldson. The wastepaper basket from under her desk, filled with trash, was carefully balanced on top of the door. A string attached to it, when pulled, would cause the basket to turn and empty its contents on the teacher's head when she walked into the room. It worked perfectly. But guess who got punished!

"Who did this?" Mademoiselle Donaldson asked.

No one moved.

The French teacher wanted the whole class—all thirteen of us—to stay after school. I raised my hand.

"Please, Mademoiselle Donaldson, I have did it. Let you me stay, yes please?"

The other girls giggled. But Mademoiselle Donaldson didn't even smile.

"Is this true?" she asked. No one answered; no one moved. I nodded my head vigorously. "Ja . . . I mean, yes."

I had to write a hundred times on the black board: *I will never be bad again.*

Next morning I was the classroom heroine.

"What did she make you do?"

"Did she whack you on the knuckles with her ruler?"

"Did you have to go to the headmistress?"

When I told them, they seemed disappointed. They turned from me in disgust. "That's all?" I heard one of them mumble. But one girl, slightly taller than the rest, came to my rescue. To this day I'll never know why.

"Leave her alone. She's a refugee. She's here all by herself."

"Aw, Prissy, we're only having a bit of fun."

"You heard me. Leave her alone," said Prissy. She put her arm around me and walked me to my desk. I had no more trouble from my classmates after that incident. Prissy saw to that.

◆ ◆ ◆

May. June. July. Still no Mama and Papa.

Then came the summer holidays. Prissy asked me: "Where are you spending the summer?"

I had wondered about that myself. Hans was in London, but he was busy working, and anyway, what did he know about eleven-year-old sisters? I shrugged. "Don't know."

"Then you're coming home with me. Miss Carter said you could."

"What about your parents?"

Prissy's eyes opened wide. "My parents? They'll agree. Of course."

Once again I had not been consulted. But this time I was happy to accept.

9

JACK

*W*e took the bus to Prissy's home in the country. Two gloriously carefree months lay ahead—months of walks in the woods; of swimming in the nearby lake; of trying to play tennis on carefully kept grass courts, though I never got any good at it. I learned to play croquet, where you had to hit colorful wooden balls with wooden mallets and make them go through wire hoops called wickets that were stuck into the lawn. I read books in English while lying in daisy-strewn meadows as the sun played hide-and-seek behind the trees. I climbed those trees, to look down into the garden and the great house at the end of the path. Day by day my English improved, without my noticing it. My skinny legs got fatter from eating fresh strawberries in thick country cream and home-baked pies filled with fruit from my hosts' own orchard, fruit which I had helped pick. Prissy's parents treated me royally. Prissy also had an older brother.

◆ ◆ ◆

Jack was seventeen. I hoped he wouldn't care that I was only eleven, but of course he took no notice of me at all. Oh, but he was handsome!

He played tennis every day, dressed in white tennis clothes. His trousers were long and neatly pressed, with a crease down the front on which you could cut your finger. His white tennis shoes were spotless, and his white shirt was open at the collar, showing off his hairy chest. He had a ruddy complexion and dark, almost black eyes. He kept having to push back his brown hair after he hit a ball. His upper lip sprouted a fuzzy chestnut mustache. It looked soft like the down of a baby chick. I wanted to touch it, but I didn't dare. He played tennis with his friends from school, who were quite nice looking, too. But I . . . oh, I had eyes only for Jack!

I would crouch against the back fence of the tennis court, praying for just a glance from him in my direction. He ignored me totally. It did not occur to me that he might have felt embarrassed by my presence. That he might have wondered: Who was this gawky little kid that kept hanging around?

Then, one day, a miracle! He spoke to me!

"Can you pick up the ball? And throw it back to me?"

Could I! My throws were weak, but I made it my mission to improve. From then on, I was Jack's slave.

❖ ❖ ❖

And during all this time, I had not an inkling of the terrible things going on in Europe, particularly in Germany. Nor did I know about the fear of mortal danger that Mama and Papa and all our friends in Germany had to deal with every day. I knew that since the Nuremberg Laws were passed by Hitler's government in 1935, Jews were considered "stateless." That was why each of our passports all had a big *J* written across the front, to indicate the word *Jude*—Jew. Male Jews of any age were forced to add the name Israel to their names, and females the name Sarah. But I did not know that Jews were being further stripped, inch by inch, of their rights, so that by now they could barely risk being seen in public anymore. They could not own or operate their businesses. Jewish doctors could no longer take care of their patients, unless they were also Jewish. The same held true for Jewish lawyers. Jewish teachers lost their jobs, and Jews were not allowed to employ non-Jews, or so-called Aryans, as domestic helpers. Jewish actors could not act unless they did so in Jewish theaters, which also ceased to exist after a time. Jewish artists could not sell their art, Jewish musicians could no longer play in German orchestras, and books written by or about Jews were burned on the streets in great public bonfires.

Worse, Jews began to disappear overnight. One day

Frau X would lean over her back fence, look over her shoulder to make sure no one else was listening, and ask Frau Y, "Have you seen Herr Z this morning?" And Frau Y would put her finger to her lips, look over her shoulders as her neighbor had done, and whisper, "They came to get him in the night." Anybody would have known whom she meant by "they." Herr Z would never be seen again. Concentration camps were spreading like a cancer all over Germany, Austria, and Czechoslovakia, and filling up fast. Not only Jews were sent there. If you practiced the "wrong" religion or were overheard to have said something against Hitler's government, or belonged to the "wrong" ethnic group, you were likely to be torn out of your bed in the night and rushed away. It did you no good to scream and call for help. No one was willing to risk his or her life to save you, especially not if you were a Jew. And it didn't matter whether you were a religious Jew or simply a Jew because your father and mother, or perhaps only your grandmother, were Jewish. Hitler wanted to rid Germany of every drop of Jewish blood. In the end, many, many drops of Jewish blood would be spilled before the madness stopped.

People in Germany, as in England, were beginning to suspect that something bad was going on. There were many rumors. There was more and more talk of war. But in the summer of 1939, who could be sure? Many Jews, and others who did not like what they saw, began to leave Germany if they possibly could. Some non-Jews tried to help their Jewish friends. But not many.

And I, in my English summer wonderland, was blissfully unaware. I rarely read the newspapers or listened to the news on the radio. Television was not around yet. The fact that the whole world was rushing headlong into global war remained of no concern to me. I had other things to occupy my mind. I was in love.

◆ ◆ ◆

When I wasn't chasing tennis balls for Jack, Prissy and I did things together, like helping her mother and the ladies at the Friends' Society. Although Prissy's father was a devout Church of England man, her mother was just as devout a Quaker.

"We are against war," she explained to me. "Quaker men will not carry arms. We think that life is too precious to kill. If they have to serve, they go as conscientious objectors."

"What's that?"

"It means they become medics or ambulance drivers, or work on farms. Anything except take another's life."

I wondered what Jack would do. But I would sooner have swallowed my tongue than ask him. At their meetings, the Friends sat in a big room in total silence. At times someone was inspired to get up and say something. Then silence followed again. I found it trying. At Miss

Carter's boarding school we were all taken to church every Sunday, including me. No exceptions. But of course I couldn't have told Prissy's mother that I did not like the Friends' meetings as much as I did the Church of England services. The elaborate ceremonies and prayers read in unison from a book seemed much more interesting. But the silence had its good points, too. It gave you time to reflect. It made you feel more at peace with yourself and the universe. After a while I began to like their way, too. I was beginning to learn that there were many ways to pray.

July meandered into August. August melted into September. Another week, and Prissy and I would have to go back to school.

◆ ◆ ◆

September 1, 1939. Six weeks had now become six months, and still no Mama and Papa.

To the west of us across the Atlantic Ocean on this day, Americans were preparing their charcoal broilers to barbecue hamburgers and hot dogs for the Labor Day weekend.

In England, on this day, we buttoned our raincoats up to our chins and pulled up our Wellingtons, which is what we called our rubber boots. Suddenly, the weather had turned gray and drizzly. Trees had turned brown overnight, dropping their dead leaves in soggy heaps onto slippery roads. The meadows smelled, not unpleasantly, of cowflops and decay. Pheasants dived into the underbrush to hide from the hunters, and geese flew honking overhead.

To the east of us across the English Channel, on this day, German soldiers goose-stepped across Germany's borders, flanked by tanks and artillery. Hitler's invasion of Poland had begun.

Two days later, on September 3, Prissy, Jack, and I were walking across the dripping field, gathering mushrooms for breakfast, as we had often done before.

"If you can peel the underside easily, like this, it's all right to eat," Prissy said. She held up a big, white mushroom and showed me again, for the sixty-seventh time, how it was done. "You have to be very careful not to pick a poison one."

Our baskets were filling up nicely.

"I'm going away tomorrow," said Jack out of the blue.

I gulped. Before either of us could ask, he explained: "I'm going into the army,"

"The army?" Prissy and I shouted in unison, and Prissy added: "Whatever for?"

So Jack didn't follow his mother's example, I thought. Too bad. I was shocked. How could he sound so eager? He would have to kill other men. He might get killed himself.

"What for?" I echoed. We had all stopped walking or

stooping down for mushrooms. How unimportant they had suddenly become. We straightened up and stared at Jack. He stared back at us, first one then the other. I knew what the answer would be.

"Don't you know?" he said. "The war has started."

10

I ALWAYS KNEW
I WAS JEWISH

*T*he mood at boarding school was gloomy after our return. For one thing, a lot of the girls hadn't come back. Some of the teachers stayed away, too. Even June was not there anymore.

"It's because of the war," we were told. "Now that our men are off to fight, women are needed on the home front. And anyway, maybe they can't afford boarding school anymore right now."

Everywhere there were patriotic posters along street walls and on public buildings. "Keep the Home Fires Burning" read one. Another showed women, looking after their households and families. But many of them were now needed in the factories to replace the men who were fighting in the war. I assumed that that, too, was meant by "home fires."

At one of our daily prayer meetings, Miss Carter told us proudly that June had joined the ATS, or Auxiliary Territorial Service. I imagined her in her smart uniform, with her little hat set rakishly to one side of her head and her thick curly hair piled up under it. Besides the young men, there were a lot of army, navy, and air force women around now, too. I wished I was old enough to be one of them.

Even though there were only a few of us left now, our lessons went on as before. Miss Carter filled in for missing teachers. In a way it was better for us, because we got a lot more attention.

Our prayer meetings were kept going, too. We sang hymns for "those in peril on the seas" and prayed to Jesus for all the brave "boys" who were fighting the evil dictator. They were not all on the seas. Planes began to fly overhead in squadrons of three or more. They flew in formation, much like the flocks of geese I had seen going south for winter. We soon learned to recognize the heavy bombers or the little one-engined fighter planes called Spitfires. Of course, jet planes were unknown at that time.

One of the less pleasant consequences of war was the way our dinner plates looked. There was much less meat on them these days, more potatoes and vegetables. We all gave up sugar in our tea, "for the war effort."

One day an air-raid warden handed each of us a funny-looking shoulder bag. They contained gas masks.

"Open up your bag and take out the mask," he said. A strange contraption that looked like a black pig's snout with an oblong window for eyes stared up at me. The black snout had little air holes in it. I was torn between a giggle and the willies. I pulled the object out of its bag and held my breath.

"Put it over your face, like this. The strap goes round the back of your head. Don't worry, just go on breathing," said our instructor.

That's easy for you to say, I thought. The smell of rubber made me gag. But after a few more practices we all got the hang of it. Gas-mask drill became part of our daily routine, right along with prayer meetings.

◆ ◆ ◆

More and more planes flew over our school. One day our air-raid warden came to tell us about the "blackout." We had to put black curtains over the windows and doors.

"Remember now. Not even a chink of light must get through in the night," he warned us. "The enemy must not see anything from above."

The enemy. That meant the Germans. My parents were still in Germany. Their letters, sent on by the Red Cross, were becoming fewer and farther between. But I knew that British planes were going over there, too, so they must have blacked out their windows just as we were doing. Of course, they couldn't have written about that. The censors would have cut that part right out. And although I certainly hoped they were looking out for their safety, I was sure Mama and Papa wanted the Allied forces to win. How stupid it was to have a war, I thought. Hitler had managed to turn the whole world upside down.

We helped our teachers and Miss Carter put up the curtains. We began having air-raid drills. A shelter was hastily put up in our play court. When the alarm sounded, we had to drop whatever we were doing and run to it. Since we never knew whether it was for real or just a drill, we ran every time we heard that awful wail. War, I decided, was not much fun.

But not all things were bad or scary. For instance, sometimes we all jumped into the back of a farmer's truck, and off we went to help with potato picking. We had fun trying to outdo one another.

"My pail has more spuds in it than yours!"

"Yah, yah, yah, that's what you think!"

"Spuds" was a slang word for potatoes.

Helping the farmers was not only a great way to help the war effort, it was also a great way for getting out of the classroom. Not only that, but we had a good excuse for getting dirt under our fingernails. Never mind that we had to write about "How I Furthered the National War Effort by Helping the Farmer." We looked forward to potato picking or whatever else we were asked to do on the farm. It was one lesson we all enjoyed.

◆ ◆ ◆

Rumors persisted.

"Hitler is going to invade England before Christmas."

"His troops are all ready to come over."

"We can't defend ourselves. Not enough men . . . weapons . . . planes . . . tanks. . . ."

Here was something else for me to worry about. The prospect of German soldiers catching up with me here in England was scary. What would they do to me? To Hans in London? Was there no escaping from the Nazis after all? I wished I could talk about this to Mama or Papa. I wished I could be with them again.

♦   ♦   ♦

My bed was one of four in my dormitory. Before the summer, all four beds in my dormitory had been occupied. Now two were vacant. Prissy found me in our room.

"Why are you staring at that picture on the wall? You look as if you'd lost your best friend," she said. She made a funny face, trying to make me laugh. I returned her question with a baleful look.

"You ever noticed the fellow with that lamb in his arms?" I asked.

"You mean the Good Shepherd?"

"Yes, the Good Shepherd."

"He's Jesus. He takes care of us as if we were his little lambs. So you needn't worry about . . ." Prissy stopped for a minute, ". . . about anything," she finished.

"But it's just a picture," I argued.

"True. It's just a picture of an idea."

I had been thinking about that. I could use a little taking care of just now.

"Do you think . . . I mean . . . does he mean me, too?" Perhaps if I didn't tell him I was Jewish, I thought, maybe he'd overlook it. Prissy looked at me funny.

"Sure. If you believe in him."

I kept studying the picture. Meanwhile Prissy was fidgeting. She hopped from one foot to another and cleared her throat several times. Finally she blurted out: "I have to leave school. Mummie wants me back home. In case of air raids or invasion."

I kept on staring at the Good Shepherd picture.

"When?" I whispered, not looking at my friend.

"Tonight. After supper. Daddy is coming to fetch me."

"Oh." I didn't know what else to say. Then I turned to her: "Are you coming back?"

She didn't answer me right away. But I knew what she would say before she said it: "I don't know."

I wished my Daddy were fetching me too. The Good Shepherd's big brown eyes seemed to be looking straight at me. He must not have noticed that I was Jewish.

◆ ◆ ◆

Children don't usually stop to analyze what's going on. But if I had, it might have gone something like this:

I had never been lucky enough to have had a solid, religious upbringing. My parents were good, kind people, but they wanted very much to be able to blend into German society. They had good reason, for Jews were not treated well during most of German history. Anti-Semitism—hatred toward Jews—was nothing new in Germany, nor elsewhere in Europe and the world. True, during the time of the Weimar Republic, formed in 1919 after the First World War, conditions for Jews in Germany eased up. There were Jews in German universities and in lower government positions. But anti-Semitism was never far away. When Adolf Hitler began slowly but surely to push President Paul von Hindenburg aside, and finally, in 1933, made sure, by tricks and treachery, of his appointment as the new chancellor, the majority of the German people were cheering for him. No wonder that my parents rejected anything that reminded them—and others—of their rich, wonderful Jewish heritage.

I was not taught about the religion into which I was born until the private German school closed its doors to me and Mama had no choice but to send me to a Jewish school. That last, sad Chanukah alone with Mama was my first introduction to Judaism. And when I came by myself to this strange, new country, learning a new language and new customs, I also learned a new religion along with everything else. For a while this new religion served me well enough. But deep down in my heart

I always knew I was Jewish. I never forgot. After all, wasn't that the reason I had to leave my home and family in the first place? Wasn't my being Jewish the one and only reason why Hitler and his Nazis wanted to kill me? But I was only eleven—too young to analyze.

11

PLEASE DON'T LET ANYTHING HAPPEN TO MAMA AND PAPA!

*D*ecember 1939. The winter holidays were coming up. Also my twelfth birthday.

The few girls that were still students at my boarding school were getting ready to leave for home. I had no prospects this time and did not look forward to being left alone with Miss Carter, the headmistress. The house, which during school term was a noisy, alive, and busy place, was suddenly turning into a tomb in which two people, a lonely girl and an old lady, were stealthily creeping around. Miss Carter used one small wing as her living quarters. We girls had often been invited to her room for Bible studies or prayer meetings. But now the idea of sitting alone with her, sweet as she was, was not a happy one. I hated holidays!

One morning, three days before Christmas, I woke up, the only girl in a dormitory for four, trying to hang on to my dream in which I was back on the roof of my house in Stuttgart. In my dream I was able to fly like a bird just by spreading my arms apart. But something, perhaps the chime of a clock, woke me. Slowly I sat up and pushed back the blackout curtain from the window next to my bed. Snowflakes as big as tennis balls—well, almost!— were drifting down from a leaden sky. Some melted the minute they reached the ground. But enough stayed to turn the world, little by little, into a white wonderland. All sound seemed muffled. On a tree branch that nearly touched my window, a lone bird sat chirping. It puffed up its feathers, then flew away. Now, nothing.

I fell back on my pillow and stared at the ceiling. Even the Good Shepherd seemed disinterested this morning. I rubbed my eyes to hold back the tears.

Then I saw it. A package wrapped in red at the foot of my bed. For me? I reached for the box and held it in my hands for a minute or so. Someone had given me a present. Who?

It could not have come from Mama and Papa. Since the war began, they couldn't even send normal letters, just some stupid Red Cross postcards, with no more than twenty-five words. They took forever to get here. Hans? His last letter to me had come from the Isle of Man, a small island in the south of England. The police had interned him there as an "enemy alien." I remembered Dachau and other concentration camps. Surely a British internment camp was not like these? Never! Impossible! I would ask Miss Carter about that. Hans had written that there were many other German Jews of his age (and older) in this predicament. Also many German non-Jews. Apparently, the British government hadn't yet learned the difference. In any case, the package could not have come from him.

The next moment I had the red paper flying all over the room. On my covers over my scrunched up knees sat a cake made of solid marzipan. My favorite! I remembered telling someone about the sweet confection made of sugar and almond paste, wishing I could have some again. I described how Mama had always given me little marzipan fruits or potatoes for my birthday. Who had bought it? Where had she found it? Surely it was a miracle, since everything from bread to beef was now very hard to find. We all had been given green ration cards. Just about everything was rationed, so that nobody would get more than anybody else. Extra rations were issued to children, but candy was considered a luxury. Surely, marzipan was the biggest luxury of all.

Before I could take out the card that would tell me who gave me this wonderful gift, the door opened softly and Miss Carter came to stand by my bed.

"Good morning, dear," she greeted me cheerfully. "Sleep well? You don't mind my coming in, do you? I'd like to talk to you."

What was wrong? Had I done something bad?

"Put on your dressing gown, it's cold today. Mind if I sit here?"

She settled herself on the edge of my bed, ignoring the

mess of red paper and my beautiful marzipan cake. I could feel it getting warm and soft under my hand.

"I'll get straight to the point. You know that most of our girls will not be back until the war is over. A lot of my teachers, too. I have to make a difficult decision, dear. I may be forced to close the school."

"Close the school? But . . ." My mouth stayed open. She sat ramrod straight. Her eyes, behind her steel-rimmed glasses, were fixed on something outside the window. Slowly she turned and patted my hand.

"Don't worry. I've taken care of you, dear. In fact, I wrote to your parents only a few days ago. I told them that I would be ready to be your legal guardian in the event . . ." She swallowed and seemed to have a hard time speaking to me. ". . . in the unlikely event, my dear, that anything should happen to them. You've heard from them not so long ago, haven't you?"

My head was spinning from all the information she had just packed into this fast-moving little speech. Even though my English was by now very good, I had trouble, this particular morning, keeping up with her.

Close the school? Legal guardian? In the event that . . . ?

"Heard from them?" I said. "Yes, I think about two weeks ago. Yes, week before last. A fortnight, I remember. The day of the exams. Arithmetic was hard, and Latin. But I did well in drawing and music." I rambled on.

"The usual Red Cross postcard, I suppose?"

"Yes. Twenty-five words. It took a long time to get here. Mama and Papa said they were coming soon. The card was sent over a month ago."

My fingers were making dents in the mushy marzipan. Miss Carter cleared her throat and dabbed at her eyes behind her glasses.

"Well, we've all been praying for them, dear. Now, about you. How would you like to spend the holidays with June's family? You know her father is my brother. They have a nice little house . . ."

"Will June be there?" I interrupted, suddenly feeling more cheerful.

"If she gets leave from the army. You can pack your things today, and tomorrow I will take you there on the bus."

She must have seen me looking, just for a second, at the Good Shepherd. "Do you like that picture, dear?" With one purposeful movement she rose and took it off the wall. "Here, dear. It's yours. Get dressed now and go down. Cook has your porridge waiting for you." She was at the door. Then she turned. "Do you like your present, dear? It's from all the teachers." Then she left. I stared after her, forgetting to close my mouth.

◆ ◆ ◆

I didn't go down right away. I sat, dressed in my robe, on the edge of my bed, fingering my marzipan. All the teachers? Wow! I took a small bite out of it. It didn't taste quite the same as it used to at home. As I chewed, I kept staring at the picture in my hand, which was now mine.

"Please, don't let anything happen to Mama and Papa," I whispered. I didn't know whether I was praying to a badly painted picture of an unlikely dressed man, or to God, or to what. I just kept saying it over and over again:

"Please don't let anything happen to Mama and Papa."

12

EVACUATED REFUGEE

We arrived in Wellingborough the next evening. Two people about Mama's and Papa's ages were waiting to greet us. A wonderful smell came from somewhere in back. It was too dark in the hallway to see where it was coming from, but it reminded me of the cookies Frieda and I used to bake at home, in Stuttgart.

"Welcome to Kirkholm," the woman said and shook my hand. "You can call me Auntie Mona. And this is Uncle Larry." She nodded her head toward her husband and went on talking. "We call our house Kirkholm. You see, we English like to give our houses names. It gives them an identity. You must have noticed that they all look alike. This street looks like any other street in any other town, and all the houses look one like the other. All semidetached. But a sign in the front somewhere that tells you what the name of this house is . . . well, it gives it a distinction, you see. 'Kirkholm' means 'Church Home.' From the Scottish. I'm part Scottish myself. The other part of me comes from the French Huguenots. They were persecuted by the Catholics and driven out of France."

I didn't know if she meant recently, the way I was driven out of Germany. But by now we were taking our coats off, and anyway, I was too shy to ask. My eyes had adjusted to the dimness and I was starting to look around.

Kirkholm was built narrow and long. A tiny garden patch, the size of a flower bed, faced the street. Although it was December, there was still one faded rose stubbornly hanging on to its long stem. The wind was doing its best to blow it down, but it clung to its stem and leaned up against the wrought-iron fence at the edge of the sidewalk. There was a little gate there. Everybody in England had a gate like that.

The front door had stained glass in it near the top, for the sun to shine through during the day. But now it was evening and getting dark. Immediately to one side was the Sunday parlor. Like all English rooms I'd seen, the parlor had a fireplace. This was probably the largest room in the house, but since this was not Sunday, the fire was not lit. I noticed an old upright piano against the wall. There was an open hymn book on the stand above the closed lid, and more hymn books were stacked on the floor. I can't wait till Sunday, I thought to myself. I loved singing hymns. My favorite was "Let Me Count My Blessings."

Across the narrow hall, opposite the Sunday parlor, was a staircase. Just under the stairs, facing the hallway, was a tiny door. I wondered what was behind it and where it led.

"It's a bit dark here," Auntie Mona laughed. "We'll have to light the gas pretty soon, Larry."

Light the gas? Whatever did she mean? Everyone had electricity, didn't they? Wrong. Not in this house. Uncle Larry saw the puzzled look on my face as I watched him reach up to the little globe inside the glass lamp on the wall and hold a long lighted match to it. A faint blue glow quickly grew into a soft yellow light. It didn't make too much difference really. At most, now, you could just about see where you were going.

"Never saw gaslight before, eh?" asked Uncle Larry. "Well now, I say this, young lady. What was good enough for my father, I say, is good enough for me. Never had much use for those newfangled inventions, is what I say. You'll get used to it, girl."

"Oh, Larry! Can't you see she's tired and hungry?" chided Auntie Mona. "Let's go in the kitchen and have a nice cup o' tea. She can see the upstairs later." A kettle was already whistling away on the stove.

I skipped behind her and Miss Carter into the kitchen as Uncle Larry quickly disappeared out the back door.

Auntie Mona asked: "Have you tasted mince pie yet?"

I shook my head.

"No? Well then, we have a treat for you. I've been baking all afternoon. Mince pies are a tradition here in England at this time of year. Sit down."

Miss Carter and I made ourselves comfortable at the kitchen table as Auntie Mona held up a big tray filled with little pies, no bigger than my hand. The spicy, fruity smell was heavenly. "Here, take one. They're still warm. It won't spoil your appetite for supper, I shouldn't think. You look like you could use some fattening up. You like it? I thought you would. Have another. Happy Christmas."

"They're wonderful, Mona," said Miss Carter. She hadn't said more than two words till now. "What kind of suet did you use? Wherever were you able to get the mince meat? Everything is so hard to come by these days, and when you do find what you're looking for, it's too expensive." They started talking about recipes and about the high cost of necessities, while I munched happily away and helped myself to more. Then came a lull in their conversation, and Auntie Mona suddenly remembered me.

"Ready to see where you'll be sleeping? Have another, first. No? Right, you'd better not or you won't have any room for your supper, will you?" She turned to Miss Carter. "You're staying, aren't you, Ellen?"

Miss Carter shook her head. "I'd best be going back before it gets too late. It's so dark these nights, what with the blackout and everything. And you never know if there's to be an air raid or not. Jerry's been flying over more and more lately. We're lucky we haven't been hit yet."

Jerry was the English nickname for the Germans.

"That reminds me," said Auntie Mona. "I want to show you where your air-raid shelter is, Olga."

"My air-raid shelter?"

"Right. We don't expect too much bombing in these parts. That's why Miss Carter brought you here. We're in the Midlands. Too far inland for Jerry most of the time. But just in case. . . . And anyway, the air-raid warden said we had to have something if we're to have children here. What I'm showing you was his idea."

To my great surprise, she led me to the little door underneath the stairs. When she opened it, I saw a tiny space, just big enough for someone my size to crawl into. "It used to be the broom storage," said Auntie Mona. I saw a mattress on the floor, made up with sheets and blankets and a pillow. It looked very cozy.

"When the sirens go off, whatever time of night, you jump into your clothes and come down here and snuggle up in this bed and go back to sleep."

"In my clothes?"

"Yes. That's what the air-raid warden said. You lay out your clothes on the chair next to your bed upstairs—I'll show it to you in a minute—so all you have to do is jump into them. The whole thing should take less than two minutes, with a little practice. You needn't wear your shoes, but bring them. And don't forget your gas mask, of course."

"Of course."

Miss Carter kissed me good-bye on my forehead and

left before supper. Uncle Larry had come back by that time, with something limp and furry hanging over the handlebar of his rusty old bike. A gun was slung over his shoulder. His cap was pulled down over his forehead, against the wind. His nose was red and dripping.

"Brought you a rabbit, girl," he sniffed. He was quite pleased with himself. "Your Auntie will make us a nice rabbit pie out of that." He sneezed and blew his nose and rubbed his hands together. "Getting a bit chilly out there."

I had never heard of rabbit pie. I wasn't sure I would like it. But I was wrong. It was truly delicious. So was everything else that Auntie Mona cooked. Though how she managed it, I'll never know. Just about everything was rationed now. With our ration cards, we could still buy a certain quantity of hard-to-get foods, such as meat and margarine. Oranges and bananas were no longer seen. Eggs were in short supply, and powdered eggs soon came to be a regular staple; also powdered milk. Children under sixteen got double rations. In that way, I suppose, I contributed to my benefactors' household. Also, the Jewish Refugee Committee in London paid Auntie Mona a small sum of money for taking me in.

But Uncle Larry, being Uncle Larry, did not rely on ration cards alone. Besides going out regularly to shoot rabbits or quail, he also tended a "Victory Garden." I will tell you about the Victory Garden in a minute. First I have to describe for you my first air raid.

As I told you, the bedrooms were upstairs. Uncle Larry and Auntie Mona had the big one in front. I soon discovered a wondrous picture hanging over their bed. I couldn't believe my eyes when I first saw that young maiden, her hair flowing in the wind, and clad in only a wisp of a shawl. She was running merrily through the woods with her beautiful Greek god, whose only adornment was the helmet on his head. Understand that Auntie Mona came from a Baptist missionary family. She was born in China. Life at Kirkholm was very strict. It centered around hymns and prayers and the Good Book. Sin was a major concern around here. But I couldn't help from sinning, try as I might. I studied that picture earnestly every time I had to go in that room. I knew I should not, but I loved that picture. It became my favorite, nearly replacing the Good Shepherd.

My own room was the next one along. It was filled up completely by the big double bed in the center. There was just enough room for a chair on each side of it, and a dresser with a washbowl and pitcher on top. This pitcher was filled with fresh water every day. I was expected to pour some of that into the bowl and wash myself each morning. There was no heat upstairs, so many a winter morning I found a thin layer of ice floating on top in my pitcher. Washing became, at most, "a lick and a promise." At night, I folded my clothes and laid them on the chair in such a way that I could jump into them at the first sound of the air-raid siren. Auntie Mona let me hang my

Good Shepherd on the wall where I could see him when I lay in my bed. There was also, under the bed, a chamber pot, made of blue and white porcelain.

There was, in fact, a bathroom down the hall. It was a complicated affair. You had to pull on a chain to flush the toilet, but you had to do it just right or it didn't work. It was freezing cold in there, as was the whole upstairs. The bathwater was heated in a boiler above the tub, which you had to turn on before you wanted to use it. Everybody took a bath once a week. Believe me, we didn't dawdle.

Two other little bedrooms snuggled up together at the back of the house. You had to walk through the bathroom to get to them. One was June's when she came home on leave from the army. The other belonged to her brother James. James was a sailor. Neither was home when I first came to live at Kirkholm.

◆ ◆ ◆

That very first night I got to experience my first air raid. I was all curled up into a ball and had just managed to warm up a spot under my mountain of blankets, talking to Mama and Papa in my head. Perhaps I had fallen asleep; it's possible. The wail of the siren brought me out of my warm nest in a second. My feet touched the cold floor before it stopped. My clothes were on me while its last groan was still hanging in the night air. Shoes and flashlight in hand, gas mask slung over my shoulder, I flew downstairs. I crawled into my shelter, and Auntie Mona came to help me fix the blankets up to my chin. Then all was quiet. I could hear her puttering about in the kitchen. I could hear her talking to Uncle Larry, and I could hear him answering her back. They both talked in low voices. My eyes were wide open, trained on the crack of light coming through a chink in the door of my cubbyhole. That gas light didn't seem as dim as before. I was glad to have it there.

Then I heard a new sound. *Brrum . . . brrrum . . . brrummm. . . .* I knew it had to be a plane. The question was, was it Jerry or one of ours? In time I was to learn the difference, just from the sound. But not yet. The Blitz of London had only just begun.

13

BONNIE AND GRETA

*T*hese daily bombing incidents were called the *Blitzkrieg,* German for "Lightning War," because the bombs fell like lightning bolts from the sky onto the people below. At the start of the Blitz, my brother Hans was living in London again, about a hundred miles or so from Wellingborough. He had been released from the Isle of Man after a few months as a war prisoner there. Travel was very much restricted, and for us to visit one another was just about impossible. Only those in the armed forces or other government people now used public railroads or buses. Cars, belonging to the privileged who owned them, slept soundly in their garages, as gasoline, or "petrol" as it was called, was in rare supply.

But even though Hans and I could not see one another, we wrote to each other regularly, once a week. Sometimes he would include news from Stuttgart, when he had it. It was always that twenty-five–word postcard through the Red Cross. The message was always more or less the same: "All is well. We will come to you as soon as possible. . . ." They were always at least two months old by the time I got them. Mama's and Papa's photographs stood propped against the washbowl on my dresser. Even so, their reality was slowly, slowly fading. Even Hans was no longer real. What *was* real was school, "the War," and surviving from day to day.

In April another girl came to live at Kirkholm. Her name was Bonnie. Bonnie was evacuated from London, along with most of her classmates, because of bombing near her school. Many Londoners began to send their children into the country through an organized effort to evacuate them. I myself was an evacuee from England's east coast, where invasion from Germany was thought to be the most likely to begin. But there was a difference between us. These London children were free to go back home any time they or their parents wanted. For me, there was no going home. What I didn't know then, but have since realized, was this: if a Nazi invasion had happened, I, as a Jew—a *German* Jew at that—would have been hunted down and killed. The fact that I was only a child would not have bothered the invaders. One-and-a-half million children who were left behind in Germany and other European countries were murdered by the Nazis during that time.

◆   ◆   ◆

Bonnie was about as old as I, though taller. We went to school together and were in the same class. To get to school, we had to walk down the hill into town and then up again on the other side, past a foul-smelling beer brewery. I held my nose every time we passed it. The boys' school was across the street from our girls' school. We never got to talk to any of the boys, which was too bad. But there was a boy in my Sunday school on whom I had a crush. The trouble was that he didn't seem to know I existed.

Bonnie and I also shared the bed. Auntie Mona put a long, skinny pillow, called a bolster, down the middle between us, and God help either of us if we moved it! We got along very well and hardly ever fought. We also shared the air-raid shelter under the stairs. I, for one, thought it fun having a sister.

Since Hans wrote to me regularly once a week, Auntie made me write back to him. He then passed my letters on to our parents in Germany, along with his. Sometimes he let them accumulate a while. I don't know which of these letters ever reached our parents. But I'm sure Mama and Papa celebrated every time they did, and I could imagine them waiting anxiously for the mailman to come again.

Hans sent me writing pads and postage stamps. He told me about the bombing in London, and about the fire watchers who had to stand on the rooftops all night on the lookout for fires. It sounded terribly dangerous, and I begged him not to do anything like that. I was glad that Wellingborough was not a prime target for the Germans.

We used to hear them going overheard on their way to London. Every time we heard them, we hoped that they wouldn't accidentally let a bomb fall on us. How ironic, I thought, that Mama and Papa had sent us both to England so we would be safe. Now even England wasn't all that safe anymore, especially London, where Hans was. But, I thought, it was still a lot safer than being in Germany. If only our parents could get away from there before it was too late!

◆ ◆ ◆

Uncle Larry used to take Bonnie and me up to his Victory Garden. We loved it there. He grew all kinds of vegetables and berries, which later Auntie Mona turned into magical meals. He also shot rabbits up there. In answer to my protests, he explained that they would eat our vegetables if he left them alone. "And anyway," he said, "they taste very good in a pie." I still felt sorry for them. But the best part about the Victory Garden was the old-fashioned carriage he had standing around up there. In olden times it would have been drawn by a team of horses. It was made of black leather and brass, which Bonnie and I kept polished and shiny. All the windows still had glass in them. Uncle Larry let us sit inside it. Although it could no longer go anywhere, we had hours of fun pretending that we were fine ladies dressed in fine clothes.

Bonnie and I went with Auntie Mona to her Baptist

prayer meetings on Sunday evenings. Once or twice they had missionaries from China speak to us. Auntie Mona was born in China, where her parents had been missionaries. The boy I liked would be there, and once he actually said hello to me. I never knew his name, but what did it really matter? Uncle Larry never came along to Auntie Mona's prayer meetings. I don't believe he went to church either.

In June I got a letter from the Refugee Committee in London. They wanted to see me in a month and would arrange for my train travel. Of course, I looked forward to seeing Hans again, but even more, I hoped they would supply me with new shoes and a coat for winter. I was growing so fast that I was sure Mama and Papa wouldn't recognize me when they saw me again. I had also put on some weight. Auntie Mona was a very good cook, though it must have been difficult, considering all the shortages and rationing. Sometimes we children were not allowed to eat the same things she ate—real orange marmalade for instance. I was jealous, but I soon forgot such trivial matters. Something far more important came along. Two things.

One, at school I acquired a new best friend named Greta, and two, James, Uncle Larry's and Auntie Mona's son, came home on leave from the navy. I detested him at first. He teased me without mercy. His hair was red like my brother's, and he was about five years older than I. After a while I got used to him and teased back. It got to be a game between us, and soon I actually enjoyed the banter. When he wore his uniform, he looked quite handsome. June, his sister, would come home now and then, too. She looked so much more grown-up than she had at school. I loved it when everybody was home, and the walls would echo with laughter.

One time I took a picture of Bonnie in front of our house with my Brownie box camera. But I snapped it in front of the house next door by mistake! Actually, since all the houses looked exactly the same anyway, I thought it didn't really matter. I sent it to Hans, and I'm sure he must have had a good laugh.

Bonnie and I also went to Girl Guides together. Girl Guides is what the American Girl Scouts was modeled on. We spent a lot of time learning to tie different kinds of knots, practicing the Morse Code, and collecting tin foil, which we rolled into a huge ball. The tin foil was supposed to help the war effort. We also talked about going to Girl Guide camp in the coming summer. I frugally saved up my sixpence (five cents) weekly allowance to buy a uniform. Our Girl Guide leader told me she had a belt that would fit me. I was thrilled! I bought the rest of the uniform piece by piece. When I was finally able to buy the last item, I felt I had accomplished something important.

The day came to keep my appointment with the people at the Refugee Committee. I took the train to London by myself, a one-day round-trip. Hans met me at the station

and went with me to the address they had sent me. They
seemed very kind. I had to fill out a form, which Hans
helped me with. Then we sat in a waiting room for a long
time. At last my name was called, and, miraculously, I
was given a new winter coat and shoes. After lunch together, Hans saw me back on the train to Wellingborough
again, and we said good-bye. We were rather formal with
one another, as if we were just acquaintances rather than
brother and sister. I remember hugging my new treasures
all the way home, and being glad that there was no air
raid while I was in London.

The war raged on. We listened to the radio and heard
that London was now being bombed day and night by
the Germans. In Wellingborough we only got one or two
hits during that time. Both occurred downtown at the
railroad station. We were told that they didn't do too
much damage.

One night, Uncle Larry let Bonnie and me stand outside by the garden gate right after the "all clear" had
sounded.

"Look up there," he told us, pointing his finger at the
horizon. "That's the city of Coventry. It's quite far from
us, maybe two hours by bike. I was there once. They
have a fine cathedral. Must have been hit badly, poor
blokes. Hope they didn't get the cathedral."

Indeed, the entire sky in the direction of Coventry
glowed an eerie orangy red. We heard on the radio the

next day that all of Coventry had been destroyed, including the cathedral.

◆ ◆ ◆

Now about Greta. This is how Greta and I became best friends. She had come to my class with the London evacuees, who swelled the population of my school to double its former size. She looked different from the other children. I could tell right away that she wasn't English. She was tall and thin. But it wasn't that. I'm not sure what it was, unless it was her hair, which was coal black, unlike all the blonde little English girls'. It stuck out from her face, making her look thinner yet. I thought she might be a refugee, like me. It turned out I was right.

Greta looked sadly through enormous brown eyes behind glasses that were so big they almost covered her face. She never smiled, and the only time she spoke was when the teacher acknowledged her raised hand. She always got the answers right. She was the exact opposite of me, especially when it came to getting the right answers!

One day Bonnie and I were walking home from school—down the hill and up the hill—when we passed Greta walking alone. On impulse I stopped, but Bonnie went on. I decided it was now or never. I watched Bonnie out of the corner of my eye, until I saw her stop and wait for me a few yards up the street.

I caught up with Greta. "Will you be my friend?" I

blurted out without preliminaries. My heart was pounding fiercely.

Greta stood still and stared at me out of those melancholy eyes, without answering. Then, with just a hint of a smile, she said: "Yes, if you'll be mine."

And that was that. In time, the three of us became inseparable. Bonnie and I learned that Greta had come from Berlin to London with her mother about the same time that I got to England, a year-and-a-half ago. Then came the Blitz, and Greta's school, like Bonnie's, was evacuated. She and her mother came to Wellingborough. I envied her for being with her mother.

"Where's your father?" Bonnie asked her.

Greta hesitated before answering: "We don't know. He was taken away . . . before we left Germany . . . to a concentration camp. . . ." And her big brown eyes grew bigger. I felt bad for having envied her.

That night I knelt by the side of my bed, as Auntie Mona had taught me, and prayed: "Please, God, let Mama and Papa come here soon. Don't let anything happen to them. Oh, and please keep Hans safe, too. Amen."

14

WHY NEW YORK?

*A*ugust 1941. Summer camp.

I was still small and skinny for my age, which was thirteen and a half. My eyes were too big for my thin face, and my pigtails did nothing to make it look fatter. My Girl Guide uniform was made of thick, dark blue cotton that clung to my skin in the summer heat. My skirt was hiked up above my knees, and I reflected with a twisted smile that if Auntie Mona could see me now, she would have a fit. At the very least she would give me one of her lectures on "ladylike behavior." But I was not being ladylike this afternoon. In fact, I was perched in a tree in the woods, with an open book propped in my lap. Auntie Mona did not approve of "wasting time just reading." But Auntie Mona was not here. I was at Girl Guide camp. Two weeks of pure fun stretched ahead in endless eternity.

Below me, a dozen or so tents sprouted like anthills beneath the trees. Most of the girls were resting inside them, lying on their cots, reading, sleeping, talking quietly. I had chosen the privacy of my favorite tree this afternoon, hiding in its broad branches and sheltering leaves. My book was called *Anne of Green Gables*, about an orphan girl my age who got a new family. I was so totally involved with Anne that at first I did not hear my name being called:

"Olga! Oh, there you are! What are you doing up there? Come down, I have something for you."

It was Mary, my troop leader. Oh oh! I thought. Now I'm in for it. I knew I was supposed to be in my tent. But she didn't seem to care. She was waving a piece of paper at me with great excitement.

"For me?" I was so surprised I nearly lost my grip on the branch.

"A telegram."

"A telegram!" I half fell, half slid down the tree. "Let me see it!" I ripped open the envelope. It was from Hans. At first the message didn't sink in. Then I felt as if I couldn't swallow, and my eyes were stinging. The whole troop had crawled out of their tents by now and crowded around me.

"What is it? Who's it from? What does it say? Is something wrong? Say something, Olga!"

But I could not. At last I managed to croak, like a frog: "Nothing's wrong. It's from my big brother in London." The girls were already starting to move away, disappointed. Then, as if from another planet, I heard myself say: "It's about my parents. They arrived safely in New York a week ago. New York. America."

I was trying to smile, but instead, tears came to my eyes. While everyone cheered, Mary put her arm around me.

"What's the matter? Aren't you happy? You look as if you'd just swallowed a lemon."

But all I could do was shrug and push her away. For a minute Mary kept her arm around me, then, with a funny look on her face, she straightened up and blew the whistle that hung around her neck: "Everyone, fall in! Chore time!"

All the girls obeyed her order, including me.

◆　◆　◆

Mechanically I picked up a broom and swept around my cot. In the kitchen tent, I peeled potatoes and carrots. Like a machine, I chopped and mixed and stirred the things that needed chopping and mixing and stirring for supper. These were the things I normally loved to do. But not today. Today, a nagging voice inside me was screaming:

Why? Why? Why New York?

I did not speak all the rest of that day and clear through supper. We ate in a long communal structure in the woods, overlooking a little stream, from where we could see the sun set. After supper we had our nightly powwow and sing-along, with the moon streaming through the branches overhead, and bright, bright stars. So beautiful. Such magic. But I could not sing.

Why New York? Why America? The question kept going round and round in my head, like a gramophone record.

I crept into my tent and got ready for bed. I sensed, more than saw, one of the girls reach out from her cot to touch me. I heard her start to say something to me, heard another girl stop her. "Leave her alone," I heard her say. "Can't you see? She doesn't feel like talking." I was grateful to her. But I said nothing.

Sleep did not come easily that night. I tossed about, rumpling my sheets and getting scratched from the wool blanket on my skin. I should be happy for them, I kept telling myself. What a selfish, ungrateful girl you are, Olga. Auntie Mona is right. She always says you should be more grateful. Haven't you been waiting all this time for them to get out of Germany? It's been over two years now. And the Nazis are killing all the Jews. They could have killed them too. They got out. So what if they didn't come here to you. We're all alive. That's all that matters. You should be happy for them.

So what's the problem? asked that voice inside me. The problem, I answered, is that for two and a half years I've been waiting for them to come *here*. And now . . . and now I don't know when we'll all be together again. Maybe never. Maybe I don't even care anymore. Anyway, I'm sick of this stupid war!

What wicked thoughts. How could I be so selfish? Please, God, forgive me. I pulled the blanket over my head, and softly began to hum a tune to myself. "There'll be peace and laughter, and joy ever after, tomorrow, when the world is free. . . ." It was a song everyone was singing those days. I must have fallen asleep, for I don't think I ever got to the end of that song.

◆ ◆ ◆

Too soon, summer and Girl Guide camp ended. School was on again. One day in October, when I got home from my piano lesson, I found a letter waiting for me. It was propped on the umbrella stand behind the front door, where the sun streamed in through the colored glass. I dropped my music on the floor and gingerly touched the envelope. I had never seen one like this before. The very thin paper was edged with red, white, and blue stripes all around. The ink looked as if it had gotten wet. But most curious were the postage stamps. On them was printed: "United States of America." I carried my letter into the kitchen and opened it carefully with a knife. I began to read:

New York, September 1941
Dearest little Ollie,
I had to smile. No one had ever called me Ollie here. And what about "little"? If only they could see how much I'd grown! *Yes,* I read, *we really are here in New*

York. I still have to pinch myself to make sure I'm not dreaming.

But getting here was not so easy. When our last papers came through, Papa and I walked arm in arm into the American consulate's office in Stuttgart. We were barely able to conceal our joy. I won't go into details now about our lives up to that day, since you left. Those times will always remain the "dark days" for me, and I don't care to think about them anymore.

The Herr Consul handed us our visas, the last papers necessary, and wished us a pleasant journey. Three days later we left Stuttgart forever. We were already on the train to Lisbon, Portugal, where we hoped our ship would be waiting, when we saw in a newspaper that the American consulate in Stuttgart had closed its doors that morning. Think of it, Ollielein! One more day and . . . ! But let me not write about that.

In Lisbon, our ship was not there. It would come soon, we were told. It took four more days. In the meantime, we had all our papers sorted out, approved, and officially stamped. When I first saw the ship that was to take us clear across the Atlantic Ocean, my heart sank. But it was afloat, and I prayed that it would remain floating. The Portuguese almost wouldn't let us aboard. They said one of my papers was missing. Papa went white with anger. In a trembling voice he demanded that they look again. We were told to wait in the waiting room. After three long hours a man came. My missing paper had been found. I nearly cried.

A week later, we saw the Statue of Liberty! We were delayed by one day, because we had an unexpected storm at sea. Everybody got sick, except me. I was so interested in the huge waves and the fabulous sky, that I didn't notice how we were being tossed about. By the time we sailed past the statue, all was calm again, and the sun was just coming up behind the skyscrapers. We were so happy, neither of us could speak. We just stood by the rail and held each other's hand. Ollie! I can't wait till you see it, too!

Now we live in a modest little apartment in uptown New York. We are learning to become Americans. Papa has a little trouble with the language. He says it sounds as if everybody has marbles in their mouths. But I seem to be picking it up quite easily. During the day, we work in the kitchen of a very fine restaurant. We prepare hundreds of grapefruits every day. At night we go to school to prepare for our American citizenship. You may not know this, but among other indignities we were subjected to by Hitler, he also left us "stateless." But why talk about that? I can't think of a more wonderful country to be a citizen of than the U.S.A. If only Oma could come here too. We are very worried about her.

I've saved the best news till last: From the first day of our arrival, we have started proceedings to get you and Hans over here too. I am sure it will not take very much longer now. Then we will all be together again. . . . Love and kisses, Mama.

Papa scribbled a few words under Mama's long letter. She hadn't left him much room. Just as well. I never could read his handwriting. What struck me was that neither of them had complained about suddenly being poor. I don't think they ever thought of themselves as poor, just temporarily not rich. In any case, they were so happy to have escaped, that nothing else really mattered.

So I should be happy, too, I told myself. The "dark days" were to be forgotten. Soon I would go to America.

15

LIPSTICK

But America was faraway, and there was still a war on. On December 7, 1941, three months after Mama and Papa had reached New York, American naval ships in Pearl Harbor, Hawaii, were attacked by Japanese airplanes. America went to war, fighting Japan as well as Germany. This ruled out all civilian travel overseas. All over the world, there were naval battles going on, as well as fighting in the air and on land. The British Prime Minister, Winston Churchill, made speeches to us over the radio. He told us that this war would cost us our "blood, sweat, and tears," but that this was "England's finest hour."

Our classes at school were constantly interrupted by air-raid warnings now. The sirens would wail, we would all drop what we were doing and line up, two by two. Then we marched out briskly to the brick shelter, to wait for the "all clear." Our nights, too, were often disturbed. Bonnie and I slept as much under the stairs as in our bed with the bolster down the middle. We could hear the planes flying over us, and prayed that they would not bomb us.

But in between these annoyances, life went on more or less as normal.

◆ ◆ ◆

I remember one time when a group of girls and I went walking in a field behind the school. We climbed a little hill, where we could sit and look into the boys' soccer field. One girl, Rita, said:

"I know where babies come from."

We all crowded around her to learn the great mystery. What she told us, in grave and solemn tones, was, I suppose, more or less accurate. But I certainly did not believe her. My mama and papa would never do a thing like that! Rita also introduced us to lipstick.

"I got it from a soldier," she boasted. All seven or eight of us passed the precious lipstick from one to the next, smearing it onto our lips as thickly as possible. Since no one had a mirror, we could only look at each other. We laughed hysterically, until somebody pointed out: "We can't go home like that. Anybody got a hankie?" One of the girls produced an almost clean handkerchief. This was passed around, too. When it came to my turn, the cloth was quite red, and I had to search for a corner that could still be used.

All the way home, Bonnie and I were frantically wiping our lips with our bare hands. "You have to get it all off," I told Bonnie. "There's still a bit over here. Auntie Mona will have a fit if she sees us."

Luckily for us, Auntie Mona was at one of her church meetings. We heard Uncle Larry puttering about in back of the house. We raced up to our room and scrubbed our mouths with soap and cold water from the pitcher, until I thought my skin would come off.

"Do you think Auntie Mona will notice anything?"

"Keep on scrubbing. There's still a smudge in the corner over there."

"She'd have a fit."

"Would she ever!"

"She's so . . ." I was groping for the right word.

"Religious!" Bonnie finished for me.

"Yes. She doesn't allow us to do anything. We can't have any fun. And she's always telling us we should be grateful."

"I know. And all we can do on Sundays is read the Bible, sing hymns, and pray. My parents are not that strict."

"Neither are mine," I said. Once again that longing came over me. It had been such a long time since I had seen Mama and Papa. Had they grown old? Had they changed, as I had? Would I ever get to America? *Was* there such a place?

"Auntie Mona is always worried about our souls," Bonnie was saying. "She's convinced we're going to rot in hell."

"Sh," I warned. "She might hear you."

"She isn't home yet, silly."

We scrubbed the last traces of lipstick off our mouths. Auntie Mona never noticed a thing.

◆ ◆ ◆

The news on the radio was bad. Jerry was bombing the stuffing out of us, and we were not winning any battles. Prime Minister Churchill kept making wonderfully emotional speeches about "fighting by land and by sea and by air" and never giving up. Just his voice alone, regardless of what he said, inspired us to do our bit for the war effort, whatever that might be. There wasn't much we could do. I never wasted any food or soap or paper. One day our wrought-iron fence was gone, gate and all. So were all the neighbors' fences, up and down the street. Iron was needed for the war. The street looked very bare without its fences.

◆ ◆ ◆

Usually we did our homework before supper. I rushed through it so I could practice the piano. I adored my piano teacher, Miss Brown. Once a week I climbed up to her little room in the school's attic. I often wondered how they could get a piano up there.

"That was quite good" was about as much praise as I could expect from Miss Brown. "Not bad. Now try to put a little more feeling into it. You've got the notes and the fingering. Hold your wrists up . . . so . . . Now, let me hear some feeling!"

I tried to please her. Handel, Mozart, Beethoven, and Bach came tripping off my fingers for her. I was entered in a contest and won third place. Mama would be very pleased. Her dream for me, before Hitler, had been that I would become a professional musician. Of course, this was out of the question now. Still, she would be pleased.

But always, Miss Brown demanded more "feeling" from me. I didn't know what she meant. Perhaps I had buried feeling way deep inside me and guarded it well, never to let any of it show. I didn't seem to have any feeling—whatever it was.

16

ANOTHER MOVE

I knew something was wrong the minute I stepped into the house. Although it was not Sunday, Auntie Mona was waiting for me in the drawing room. The house was empty. But before I could ask her where Bonnie was, she sat me down in front of her and, true to her nature, came right to the point.

"The people at the Jewish Refugee Committee in London think you should live closer to school. Their letter came today. And quite honestly, Uncle Larry hasn't been feeling too well lately, and I'm a bit tired these days myself, to tell you the truth."

Though the words tumbled out of her mouth, they didn't sound like the truth to me. But all I managed to say was: "And what about Bonnie?"

"She's going home to London soon. Her mum and dad want her back."

"What about the bombs?"

"I know . . . but they're nice people you're going to.

You'll come and visit me here. Once a week, all right? We'll have tea together. Thursdays all right? You won't forget to read your Bible, will you?'' She sounded ill at ease. I thought she was holding something back from me. But what?

Obediently and in silence I collected my things. Once again, no one had bothered to ask me. If they had, what would I have answered? I wondered what Mama and Papa would say if they were asked. I knew they were trying to get my visa so that I could come to America. There was a part of me, a part I hardly dared admit even to myself, that wanted to stay right here in England. Life at Kirkholm wasn't so bad. I liked Uncle Larry, and when June and her brother came home it was always a lot of fun. The problem was Auntie Mona. It wasn't that she was not kind to me. I knew she was doing her best. She was just awfully strict and unsmiling. So different from Mama. And when it came to religion, she was completely unrelenting. The fact that I was Jewish didn't concern her in the least. I had all but forgotten it myself.

◆ ◆ ◆

My new foster parents, Uncle Albert and Auntie Millie, lived across town, five minutes away from my school. But it might as well have been five hours, or five days, for all the times I now had to be absent.

Uncle Albert worked in a local shoe factory. I remember him best with his pipe clenched between his teeth and a smile frozen on his clean-shaven face. He was gentle in contrast to Uncle Larry's blustering, clumsy ways. His body was slight compared with Uncle Larry's large-boned frame. Uncle Albert wore his threadbare clothes with a flare, while Uncle Larry's always looked as if they just had been picked out of a rag bag. Uncle Albert spoke softly and treated me gently. Uncle Larry's feelings were hidden behind a gruff surface. I missed Uncle Larry a lot.

Auntie Millie was another story.

"One thing you should know right from the start," she said almost at once. "We are not church-going folks, and we don't expect you to be. All this praying and God stuff isn't good for you. It can make you mean and crazy."

I stiffened. Auntie Mona and Uncle Larry were not mean and crazy, I told myself. I liked going to church and prayer meetings, and hearing missionaries and singing hymns. What else was reliable and constant in my life? Surely, I thought, people are not reliable or constant— not even my own mother and father. Hadn't they promised me they would come to England? And hadn't they gone to America instead? But suddenly I had a new insight. I thought I understood what it was Auntie Mona had been holding back from me. The Jewish Refugee Committee had wanted me to move again because they thought I was getting too much church. Funny that they had waited so long. But, I thought, they must have been very busy keeping track of all the other refugee children from the *Kindertransport*. After all, I was only one of many.

Without looking at me, Auntie Millie went on talking a mile a minute:

"And another thing. I'm not a well lady. Some days I may ask you to stay home from school and do for me. I got arthritis." And she went into a long speech about her affliction.

She did look a little sickly to me. On second thought, I felt sorry for her. Still, I wasn't about to miss Auntie Mona's prayer meetings. Missing school now and then— I had no problem with that! But Auntie Mona's prayer meetings? No. I didn't want to upset Auntie Mona. What kind of gratitude would that have shown?

As it turned out, I had to stay home sooner than I expected, but not because of Auntie Millie's arthritis.

"Why on earth are you scratching yourself so much?" she asked me one night.

"I have something wrong here. A rash."

"Show me."

I pulled down my sock and stuck out my leg. It was covered with red, itchy circles, about an inch in diameter.

"Oh my heavens! If it doesn't look like ringworm. Do you have it anywhere else?"

I bared my other leg, my arms, my still flat-as-a-pancake chest.

"What about your head? Let me see. Yep. You got it there, too. Ringworm all right."

I had to take pills and wash with a special sort of soap. I found out that I had a kind of fungus, which I most likely had caught from the dog. It was highly contagious. No school for me. It took over a week to clear up.

◆ ◆ ◆

Most of the girls in my class had started their periods by now. One after the other would come in and proudly tell the rest of us: "Can't go to gym today. Got it this morning."

I was fiercely jealous. Here I was, almost sixteen, and not a sign of anything. My breasts were as flat as a boy's, my hips as straight. I was convinced I was a freak.

But one morning I woke up and my pajama bottoms had a little blood on them. I jumped out of bed and ran into the kitchen.

"Auntie Millie!" I yelled. "I got it! I got it!"

Auntie Millie held her tea cup in midair. "What have you got?"

"It," I said, pointing with importance to my pajama bottoms. She caught on immediately. But my joy at not being a "freak" anymore was quickly squelched.

"Shhh!" Auntie Millie set down the teacup and put a finger to her lips. "It is not something we talk about. You mustn't give the show away." And she showed me what to do.

Funny, I thought. Ringworm I was allowed to talk about. My period I was not. Ringworm I had felt ashamed of. The other I was immensely proud about. Was this ever an upside-down world?

♦ ♦ ♦

Auntie Millie got sick just before Christmas. Her legs hurt so much that she needed a cane to walk. They got worse and worse. Finally she couldn't get out of bed anymore. I stayed home and "did" for her. It was exam time. I would have to make up for it.

Her daughter, Megan, came home from the army on a twelve-day leave. Auntie Millie felt better, but still not terrific. Megan was cheerful and brought some life into the house. She slept in my bed, and we got along well. But all too soon she had to go back to the war again, right after my birthday. Our dreary life went on as before.

I hated school more and more. I did very poorly on my exams. I remembered that in Stuttgart I had been an excellent student. Even back in boarding school in Norwich, when I first came to England, I was still a good student. What had happened? Miss Carter, the headmistress there, still showed some interest in me through letters to her sister-in-law, Auntie Mona. But they had little effect on me. Since coming to Wellingborough, my studies had slipped. I thought that this might have had to do with my moving around so much. I was really never sure if I would be staying in one place for long. Certainly, staying home to take care of Auntie Millie, thus missing exams, didn't help any. Another reason might have been that no one here was really all that interested in my schooling or in helping me with homework. Except for Miss Carter, none of my benefactors had had much schooling themselves. So how could they help me? Also, there were no guidance counselors in schools then. I had no one to turn to with my problems, and I felt I was on my own when it came to my education. I didn't even know I *had* problems.

An idea began to form in my head.

◆ ◆ ◆

One night I informed Auntie Millie and Uncle Albert: "I'm leaving school."

We were sitting by the fireplace. I had been struggling with a math problem. After I had dropped this bombshell, I jumped up and started poking the fire. Auntie Millie stopped knitting. All you could hear was the crackling wood in the fireplace. Uncle Albert chewed on his pipe and dropped his newspaper.

"Leaving school?" they said in unison.

"You don't have to go once you're sixteen," I explained.

"But you didn't finish yet," Auntie Millie said weakly.

I shrugged. "I know." I kept on poking the fire, sending great sparks up the chimney. One flew out onto the carpet. I quickly stepped on it.

"What do you have in mind to do?" asked Uncle Albert.

I shrugged again. "Don't know. Be a baby nurse, maybe. I like children."

"What will your parents say?" Auntie Millie asked.

For the third time I shrugged my shoulders. "Don't know."

◆　◆　◆

A couple of months later I found out what my parents had to say about my wanting to leave school. It took our letters that long to cross the Atlantic Ocean back and forth, because of the war.

". . . Papa and I are absolutely against it. You should finish your education," I read. But then Mama added something that was to direct the rest of my life, though she may not have intended it. "But we are very faraway from you," she wrote in the very next sentence. ". . . and in any case we believe that you are old enough to have a mind of your own. If you really insist on leaving school before your graduation, then we cannot stop you. If you want to be a baby nurse, then at least get the very best training available. . . ."

I showed Mama's letter to Auntie Millie.

She looked puzzled. "I think I'll write her a letter," she said. And she did. It was a great effort on her part, but it was too late. My mind was made up. Although my brother was also against my leaving school, I had already commissioned him to find out about a nursing school in London. As to who would pay for it, I gave this not a thought. Somehow I would manage.

And then I met Mrs. Wolton, and once again, everything changed.

17

A JOB!

I was sipping my sugarless tea in Auntie Mona's kitchen. It was Thursday, my usual visiting day. I had mixed feelings about visiting Auntie Mona. Part of me wanted to come back to the house that had been home for over three years. The other part of me was slipping away from her strict Baptist rules. Today had already gone off on the wrong foot, right from the start.

"Someone saw you at the cinema last week, Olga," said Auntie Mona straight out.

I stared at the grayish brown liquid sloshing around in my teacup. I had half expected this.

"On Sunday!" continued Auntie Mona, like a relentless toothache. I kept up my interest in tea.

"Well, what have you to say? Does Sunday mean nothing to you any longer? Have you forgotten so soon?"

For a second I looked up to see her eyes actually well up. Quickly I lowered mine again.

It was perfectly true. Megan, home on a short weekend leave, had invited me to go with her to see *Bambi*.

"But it's Sunday," I had objected, without much conviction. "I'm not supposed to go to the movies on Sundays."

"Oh, bother Sundays!" Megan had laughed off my guilt. "And anyway, who will see you?"

Someone evidently had and had gone straight to Auntie Mona to report me. Just as I was preparing my self-defense—I had loved the sad but funny Walt Disney movie—the doorbell rang, and Auntie Mona jumped up to answer it. She was gone for a few minutes. When she came back, she was all smiles. It was as if the sun had suddenly come out from behind the thunderclouds.

"There is someone outside whom I think you would like to meet," she said. My sin seemed forgiven, perhaps forgotten.

"Who is it?"

"Come see. Better put your jacket on, it's a bit nippy out today."

A tall, thin woman stood where the garden gate had once been. Her eyes were dancing behind her glasses, as if they knew a joke they wanted to share with us. She was holding on to a baby carriage. I was most impressed with her attire. Instead of a coat or jacket, she wore a colorful shawl about her big shoulders, and her long legs were ensconced in thick woolen stockings. Laughing with obvious pleasure, she invited me to inspect the baby carriage.

"It's twins!" I shouted. I couldn't take my eyes off them.

"Yes. Two boys. Charles and Douglas. They just had their first birthday," their mother informed us proudly.

"Oh, they are beautiful!" I said, then blurted out: "I want to be a baby nurse, you know."

"Well, what luck! I've been looking for someone to help me. There are four other children in our house. Well, three actually. The oldest boy is away at boarding school now."

Auntie Mona joined in: "This lady is Mrs. Wolton, our neighbor. Her house is at the top of this street, Olga, the one going across. It's the big house with the circular driveway." She paused for a minute, then said: "Do you think you would like to work for the Waltons?"

Without a moment's thought I answered:

"Would I!"

♦ ♦ ♦

Later that evening I sprang my news to Auntie Millie and Uncle Albert. I must admit, they were less enthusiastic than I.

"But I thought you wanted to go to nursing school?" Uncle Albert reminded me.

"I did," I assured him. "But this is much better. I'll get experience while doing the work and get paid for it.

Mrs. Wolton is so nice. Her husband is headmaster of the boys' school." I saved the best part for last: "And I'll be able to stay right here in Wellingborough. If I get a day off I'll visit you. Of course," I added soberly, "I'll have to visit Auntie Mona and Uncle Larry, too, sometimes. I'll be right around the corner from them."

◆ ◆ ◆

I earned two shillings and sixpence a month—about five dollars. It was a lot of money to me. I saved some of it toward my bicycle fund. But most of it I spent on licorice candy or an occasional movie. Hans, to whom I still wrote faithfully once a week, supplied me with postage stamps and writing paper, as well as news from America, when there was any. My clothes came mostly from the Jewish Refugee Committee in London. I needed little else.

I soon found out that I no longer needed to save money for a bicycle, because I could borrow Mrs. Wolton's bike anytime she didn't need to use it herself. I rode it across town, down the hill, and up the hill on the other side when I visited Auntie Millie.

"What's it like at the Woltons'?" she asked. "Tell me about it. Have another apple tart. I made them for you this morning. Well? Do you like it?" She sounded as if she had actually missed me.

"I love it." I assumed Auntie Millie meant how do I like my new job. I bit into the sweet, spicy tart and continued talking with my mouth full. "It's great fun. So many people! Let's see, there's Carol, she's the oldest girl, almost eight. Then there's Ann Marie, she's five. And Irene who is only three and a half. She's the naughty one. May I have another tart? And, of course, the twins, Charles and Douglas. And . . ."

"There are more?" Auntie Millie forgot to close her mouth.

"Oh yes. Let me see. There's the nanny, Emily. I help her with everything. I really love her. And a Mrs. Alford and her little girl, Fay. Fay's father is in the war, and Mrs. Alford is living with the Woltons because she doesn't want to live in London right now. The Blitz, you know. I think Mr. Alford is a captain in the army."

"How old is little Fay?"

"About as old as Irene. But the two are not a bit alike. They quarrel a lot. Irene is always getting into trouble. Everybody thinks Fay is a good girl, but she's really a bit sneaky."

"Sounds noisy to me," said Auntie Millie, and she pursed her lips.

I ignored her. "It's a huge house. Lots of rooms. Then there are the armed service boys. They keep popping in and out. We never know when one of them might show up. They come whenever they get leave."

"British boys?"

"Mostly. And Americans, too." I neglected to tell her that I already had a crush on several of them. I was sure she wouldn't have understood.

♦ ♦ ♦

Every day on the radio, we heard about air raids over London and Berlin, of battles on the high seas, of invasion landings in France and elsewhere. In Poland, as we were to find out later, thousands of Jewish people were being forced by the Nazis to live in small, walled-in areas, called ghettos. This made it easier for the Nazis to round them up, like cattle, and—like cattle—to herd them into railway cars. They were taken to "extermination camps," where they were brutally killed—women, men, and children, too. The Jews of Warsaw, Poland, and of other ghettos tried to fight back, but the Nazis had more weapons and overpowered their resistance. Millions of Jews and other "undesirables" were being slaughtered in Hitler's death camps, with few words about it from our newspapers or radios. These things were happening only a few hours' travel time from Wellingborough. But, while we were certainly aware of *some* of the horrors of the war, no one could have known the whole truth. There still was laughter and music and the sound of children's voices and the good smells of cooking, despite the scarcity of certain foods. The house I now lived in, the Woltons' house, was filled with life and love.

I stopped visiting Auntie Mona on Thursdays and going to church on Sundays. I rarely biked across town to drink tea with Auntie Millie and Uncle Albert. My picture of the Good Shepherd got tucked away in a drawer, under my socks and blouses. Soon I forgot about it. I was too busy with the children, whom I adored.

Once, Hans came down from London to see me. He seemed like a stranger to me, and I think he was as glad as I when the visit was over.

Although a few got lost, due to the war, some letters from America reached me. Mama and Papa were working hard, they wrote. They longed for the family to be together again. They were doing everything possible to obtain the papers necessary for my brother's and my immigration, but the war slowed all progress. I don't know about Hans, but I was in no rush. Yes, I wanted to be with my parents again. But my life was now in England, and I was content to stay there, forever if need be. Slowly, I had begun to sink roots in another country, another culture. Stuttgart was fading away, as a dream forgotten.

News had reached Mama and Papa that Oma, my grandmother, had gone on a "journey east." They knew, they wrote, that this could mean only one thing. Concentration camp. Dimly I remembered my grandmother at the station, waving goodbye and handing me a small present—the dictionaries. At that time all I could say in English was "the dog is under the table." How surprised she would have been to learn that now, only six years later, I had forgotten nearly all my German.

For me, the war had become a way of life. Not since

Greta had I seen another Jew. I never thought about it. Despite everything, I was happy. For one thing, no one at the Woltons' ever told me that I had to be grateful.

◆ ◆ ◆

And then, almost a year since I'd come to work here, I got the letter for which I'd been waiting all this time, with so much hope, and so much dread.

New York, U.S.A.   March 1945
Dearest Ollie,
Good news! We have your visa. Come to America. . . .

18

SAILING TO AMERICA

*T*ime to leave. Tears flowed. My ribs were sore from all the hugs. Mrs. Wolton traveled with me to the ship in Swansea, Wales, by way of London. In London, at one of its finest department stores, she bought me a suit. It was to last me for many years.

In Swansea, we cried again.

"I don't want to leave!" I wailed.

"Neither do I want you to, darling. But your parents have waited for you long enough. One day you will come back," she promised, trying to smile. I sniffed and looked away.

The ship was an old freighter modified to take on a few passengers. We sailed on a cold, rainy day in April. The sea was rough. To me, it looked unfriendly. And I was right. But this was not altogether due to the waves. It had mostly to do with the war. Because one ship alone on the ocean would have been vulnerable, we picked up a convoy along the way. This meant other ships of various

sizes and builds, including naval vessels, zigzagged back
and forth across the ocean together. At times, when the
clouds lifted, we could see one another in the distance.
Just knowing we were not alone made us all feel a little
safer. Because our speed had to conform to that of the
slowest ship in convoy, it took thirteen days to cross.
During that time, we did have at least one torpedo scare,
but nothing came of it. The sea was stormy almost all the
way. Sometimes the furniture slid from one side of the
room to the other, and dishes flew.

After thirteen days, we docked in Halifax, Canada. I
was glad to step onto solid land, land that didn't move
under my feet.

From Halifax, we rode south to New York on a Pull-
man sleeper. I had a little compartment that converted
into a bed by night. A conductor came around to make
up the beds. By day it became a regular train seat again.

After three days and three nights, we pulled into Grand
Central Station, New York. Eagerly I peered through the
window. Last stop. America!

I jumped off the train, adjusted my pillbox hat, hitched
up my shoulder bag, straightened my back, and strode
purposefully down the long, crowded platform. So many
people! My heart was racing madly. My mouth felt suddenly dry, the palms of my hands sweaty. It had been six
years. Would I recognize Mama and Papa again? And
how would I ever find them in this crowd? For a moment
I saw myself six years earlier, a skinny kid with pigtails,

waving good-bye to Mama and Oma from the *Kinder-transport* train, the train that took me away from Germany forever. How long ago it all seemed! In England I had been so engrossed with my own everyday life that I hadn't given much thought to Oma. Then came the news that she had been taken "east," to the dreaded concentration camp. For the first time in six years, I missed her. I wished I could talk to her again. Hear her voice again. . . .

Then, suddenly I saw them! They were walking toward me, their eyes darting left and right, searching, searching. I spoke first: "Hello, Mama! Hello, Papa!"

They stopped and stared at me. For a minute no one spoke. All sound ceased. The crowd became as shadows, silently passing by in slow motion. Then Mama found her voice.

"Ollie! Is it you? Are you Olga?"

Suddenly, the last six years in England melted away. I was safely in the arms of my parents again.

AFTERWORD

*F*ifty years after I had left Germany with the *Kindertransport* in 1939, I was again on a journey from London to New York. This time I traveled by air. It was not my first time since I had left England in 1945. I had been back often to visit the Wolton family, as they had visited me in America. But this time something was different. This time, I was coming back from a fiftieth reunion of the *Kindertransport*.

Two thousand people had attended, two hundred of them from the United States. Now, on my way home, I was still filled with excitement. After so many years, some of my questions had been answered at last. For one thing, I had always assumed that I was one of a few hundred children of this unique rescue operation. To my surprise I learned that I had been one of *ten thousand*!

As I sat on the plane, flying across the now peaceful Atlantic Ocean, I thought about how things had turned out for me. Miraculously, mine is a story with a happy ending. One of the terrible things I found out at the two-day reunion was that of the ten thousand children, nine thousand never saw their parents again. Others never saw their brothers or sisters again. Just about all had lost cousins, uncles, aunts, a friend, a neighbor—someone—in that murderous time in history, now called the Holocaust.

I was one of the lucky ones. Not only was my life saved, but so was that of my brother and my parents. My grandmother was not as lucky. Shortly after the war ended, in April 1945, we found out that the Nazis had murdered Oma in a concentration camp in Terezin, Czechoslovakia. The Germans called it Theresienstadt.

This is what we were told, partly by Tante Nelly, Mama's sister, and partly by Lilo, her daughter:

Oma managed to stay in her own house in Wiesbaden until some time in 1943. By then she was quite old and already weak from hunger. When the Nazis came to drag her away, Tante Nelly and her husband, Onkel Julius, were taken along with her. I remembered the news we got that Oma was "going on a trip east." We had never been quite certain what it had meant. Now we learned that many others had received similar news from loved ones in Europe. There is no longer a doubt. They were code words for what really took place.

Eventually, Tante Nelly and Onkel Julius escaped from Theresienstadt by getting on the wrong train. Years later, on one of my visits to London, my cousin Lilo told me about it:

Every day the freight trains of cattle cars would stand on the tracks waiting to be loaded with their human cargo. Although none of the people knew, they were going to Auschwitz, another notorious concentration camp, where gas chambers and ovens were waiting to kill all who came there. But on this day, Tante Nelly saw two trains, and the second one was a regular passenger train.

She was ordered by the Nazi official to board that one. With unbelievable courage, Tante Nelly defied her tormentor by demanding that Onkel Julius come with her. What made them agree to it? We'll never know. But the two were hastily pushed into that second train, and with shades drawn over the windows—on strict orders—they sped away from that dreadful place. They had no idea where to. They were fearful that it might be to another camp. Another place of suffering and death.

When they could open the shades again, they saw that they were in Switzerland.

Switzerland was a neutral country during World War II. On that day the Swiss happened to have made an agreement with Hitler: Switzerland would be allowed to take in a few Jews if the Swiss government paid the Nazis a large sum of money. Hitler needed cash. My uncle's and aunt's lives had been bought by the Swiss. In due time they were to become Swiss citizens.

But Oma had died in the concentration camp. Herr and Frau Gumpel, our former neighbors in Stuttgart, had also been killed.

* ◆ ◆

Hans, being of military age during the 1940s, could not get his visa to America yet. Nor could he get permission from the British to leave England. In fact, soon after the onset of war, in 1941, the British government decided to intern all German-born men and women of military age. They did not discriminate between Jews and non-Jews. Anyone, they thought, might have been a spy or a collaborator. Hans was one of the many young men deported to the Isle of Man, a small island off the southern coast of England. Others, including another uncle of ours, were shipped off to Australia or Canada. They were not mistreated, but there is no getting around the fact that they were imprisoned. In less than a year, however, the authorities must have realized their mistake. They let the Jewish Germans out. Hans returned to London and worked in a war productions factory. He was still not able to leave the country and had to wait until 1946, after the war, to join Mama, Papa, and me in New York.

◆ ◆ ◆

As soon as I arrived, I was told that I must finish school and get my high school diploma. I did manage it, though I had to repeat my senior year. I had failed American history. I went to work right after graduation. In 1948 I met my husband, Rolf, and was married in 1950. When our three children grew old enough to ask questions, I began to explore my Jewish heritage. I have been exploring it ever since. In June 1991, when I was 63, I celebrated my own Bat Mitzvah.

◆ ◆ ◆

The 1989 reunion in London, organized by a former *Kind*, whose name is Bertha Leverton, was a turning point in my life. The idea to write a book about my childhood, *for children*, first came to me there. I looked around the huge gym hall where the speeches were held, prayers offered, meals served, concerts given, and saw a roomful of elderly and aging people. Most of us were still agile and vigorous. But how many years did any of us have left? I needed to tell my story and tell it now.

Fifty years had gone by since *Kristallnacht*. The Night of Broken Glass took place on the night of November 9–10, 1938. Fifty years had passed since a small group of brave people hastily organized the *Kindertransport* to save the children. It took much negotiation, superhuman effort, and even an act of parliament in England. The first trainload of one hundred children left Germany on December 3, 1938. The last train was sent out at the end of August 1939, a few days before Hitler started World War II, on September 1. After that, there could be no more trains filled with children.

Ten thousand children between the ages of four months and seventeen years had been rescued. Many were left behind. Some managed to escape by other means. The majority were killed.

◆ ◆ ◆

I sat on the plane on my way home from the reunion and thought about all this. I thought about how lucky I was. I thought about the millions of refugees still roaming the world today—many, too many of them, children. I knew how bewildered and frightened they must feel. I had been there myself. I knew that what they need, more even than shelter and food, is love and understanding. As I looked back to my childhood, I realized that these two, love and understanding, are the most difficult to give to a child not your own.

The English families who took care of me did the very best they could. Under trying circumstances, they were enormously kind to me. I'm sure I didn't always deserve their kindness, nor was I always as grateful as I was asked to be. But because they were not my parents, they could not show me the love that I craved. The one exception was the Wolton family.

Today I feel myself part of that family. We have visited each other many times. My children have come to love them as much as I. In her eighty-third year, Mrs. Wolton came to America to attend my daughter's wedding.

As I write this, another war is raging across the sea, in the Persian Gulf. Among all the other casualties, the children of that area will be suffering too. Many thousands of them will be refugees. I hope and pray that they will be taken care of by strangers, as I was, even if they profess another religion. And that other children, when they have the chance to get to know them, will be kind to them— as were many of the children who met me, though not all. But most of all, I hope and pray that a day may come soon when there will be no more need for people to become refugees.

My parents died of old age, in America, many years ago. I thank them, in particular Mama, who had so much courage and foresight in sending her little girl across the sea to safety and survival. I hope and pray that future mamas, the world over, will never have to make such decisions again.